PASTELS
MASTERCLASS

Judy Martin

PASTELS
MASTERCLASS

LEARNING FROM PROFESSIONAL ARTISTS AT WORK

HarperCollins*Publishers*

ACKNOWLEDGEMENTS

*The author would like to thank the following
manufacturers and distributors for supplying
information about their pastel products:
ColArt UK/Conté, Daler-Rowney,
Faber-Castell, Rexel/Derwent, H. W. Peel/Sennelier,
Frisk/Talens Rembrandt, Unison. Many thanks also
to Jon Wyand for photographing the
demonstration sequences on pages 52–3, 84–5 and 101;
to Diana Constance and Sally Strand for
photographing their own demonstrations;
and to Cathy Gosling, Caroline Churton and
Caroline Hill at HarperCollins.*

First published in 1993 by
HarperCollins Publishers, London

© Judy Martin, 1993

Judy Martin asserts the moral right to be identified
as the author of this work.

**A CIP catalogue record for this book is available
from the British Library**

Art Editor: Caroline Hill

ISBN 0 00 412662 9

Set in Optima and Weiss
by Wearset, Boldon, Tyne and Wear
Colour origination by Colourscan, Singapore
Printed and bound in Hong Kong

PAGE 1: Diana Constance,
Victor, 680×500 mm
($26\frac{3}{4}$×$19\frac{3}{4}$ in)

PREVIOUS SPREAD: Geoff
Marsters, *Fen Landscape*,
480×660 mm (19×26 in)

CONTENTS

INTRODUCTION 6

MATERIALS 8

TECHNIQUES 14

INTERPRETING THE SUBJECT 20

MASTERCLASS *with Diana Armfield* 28

MASTERCLASS *with John Blockley* 38

MASTERCLASS *with Tom Coates* 48

MASTERCLASS *with Diana Constance* 58

MASTERCLASS *with Margaret Glass* 68

MASTERCLASS *with Debra Manifold* 78

MASTERCLASS *with Geoff Marsters* 88

MASTERCLASS *with Ken Paine* 98

MASTERCLASS *with Sally Strand* 108

MASTERCLASS *with Frances Treanor* 118

ARTISTS' BIOGRAPHIES 128

INTRODUCTION

The unique value of a masterclass is that it teaches practicalities from within a personal context. It is not a formalized lesson based on assumptions about what the student needs to know, but a direct insight into the working methods of the professional artist. The ten artists contributing to *Pastels Masterclass* represent a wide range of style, subject matter and technique. In discussing their ideas and approaches, they pass on much valuable information about handling pastels and making the most of the beautiful colours and responsive textures of different pastel types. At the same time, they convey a fascinating impression of the day-to-day realities of creative work – the processes of thinking things out and applying technical skill and control, while remaining open to experimentation, momentary inspiration or happy accident.

Painting and drawing are open-ended activities. There are no absolute guidelines about what to do, where to start or how to progress. It is possible to learn some basic elements of technique and composition, but these do not exist in a vacuum; they have to be applied to something – an observation from the real world or a picture in your head. No one can tell you the right way to do this, because your own interpretation is what counts; but they can offer you the benefit of their experience.

I am grateful to the contributors for sharing their knowledge and experience in this way – it does not always seem easy or desirable to give away the expertise that has been earned by hard work, trial and error. When an artist consistently achieves a very high standard of work, as all these contributors do, it is tempting to assume that he or she has passed some sort of 'pain barrier' and left the failures and disappointments behind. It has been especially interesting to discover how little the masterclass artists take their skills for granted and how fresh their approaches remain. They are aware that there is always something else to know; that what works today won't necessarily work tomorrow. But they also convey the immense amount of pleasure to be had from exploring a medium so thoroughly and learning to use it so well.

You may be able to identify basic principles and techniques that the masterclass artists have in common, but primarily it is the great variety they achieve with pastels that provides the excitement and inspiration. To come into a masterclass means starting at the top of the range – it encourages ambitious thoughts; but I am confident that the information provided here is valuable both to the newcomer to pastels and to more practised artists who have not yet discovered the full potential of this medium. As a working artist, I have learned something from each of the contributors that has been immediately useful, and I thank them for stimulating those new thoughts and skills. As a writer, I also thank them for their wise and funny words; they have articulated the problems and rewards of their work with enthusiasm and humour. It has been a privilege and a delight to represent them in this book and to share their enjoyment of the medium of pastel.

Judy Martin

MATERIALS

Every brand of pastels has particular qualities – there is no absolute standard for either texture or colours – and every artist finds out by experimentation which types are best suited to individual style and technique. Few artists use one brand exclusively; they may pick from several kinds to build up a palette of selected colours.

The properties of a pastel depend on the basic ingredients of pigment and binding medium. Soft and hard pastels are usually bound with natural or synthetic gums or resins; oil pastels with oils and waxes. An inert filler may be included to improve handling qualities, bulk out the paler tints, and give opacity to naturally translucent pigments. Soft and oil pastels are commonly sold in paper wrappers, which protect the sticks until they are put to use; the outer layer of the pastel may also have a fine 'skin' of binding medium that needs to be broken down with a quick, hard stroke before the colour begins to flow easily from the tip or the edge of the stick.

Storing materials
Pastels are relatively fragile and the sticks easily become dirty from the mixing of loose dust and fragments. The ideal way to store them is in sturdy trays or boxes, laid out in rows rather than jumbled together

SOFT PASTELS

Soft pastel is the medium of traditional pastel painting techniques, but can also be used for linear drawing. The pastels are made with the minimum of binder required to hold the pigment in stick form. Textures vary subtly in the smoothness and graininess of the stroke; combining different textures can be helpful in techniques that involve layering the colours heavily. The sticks are usually round in section; standard size is about 8 mm ($\frac{3}{8}$ in) in diameter, but some manufacturers produce sets of large pastels up to 32 mm ($1\frac{1}{4}$ in) thick. Soft pastels provide the most extensive colour ranges of all the pastel types: generally, good-quality brands provide a minimum of 100 colours and the largest ranges include several hundred hues, tints and shades.

HARD PASTELS

These are similar in composition to soft pastels but an increased quantity of binder gives the sticks a harder, more incisive texture suitable for drawing in line and applying linear techniques such as hatching and crosshatching. The sticks are usually square-sectioned and about 8 mm ($\frac{3}{8}$ in) thick. There are fewer brand-name products and the colour ranges are limited in comparison with soft pastels, but they are a useful adjunct for sharpening the detail in a composition and elaborating surface textures.

▲ Soft pastel marks
Although the texture of soft pastel is very giving, it is a versatile medium with effects that vary from sharp lines and flourished strokes to dense layering and glazing of the colours

▶ Soft pastel colours
One of the most frequently mentioned reasons for choosing soft pastel over other media is the wide range of beautiful colours and the intensity of hues and tones

◀ Hard pastels
In this landscape detail hard pastel has been laid over soft to sharpen the forms and textures and introduce strong colour variations. The finer, harder pink and orange strokes in the foreground and on the tree trunks are done in hard pastel

OIL PASTELS

The oily binder creates a juicy texture; because of the moistness, colours remain movable on the working surface. The colour range is relatively restricted, typically about 50 colours rather than hundreds; the hues tend to be less subtle and there are fewer variations of tone. Because of this, many artists find the oil medium less versatile than soft pastel, but it has rich characteristics and also combines interestingly with dry pastel colour. A few manufacturers produce limited ranges of giant oil sticks, which have the fluid texture of oil paint.

Oil pastels
This medium is highly manipulable. The textures vary from light glazes to substantial impasto strokes which, because the colour remains movable on the surface, blend and mesh sympathetically

PASTEL PENCILS

These are fine, hard pastel sticks encased in wood, typically used for adding detail to work in soft and hard pastel, rather than as a drawing medium in their own right, although they can be handled in just the same ways as other kinds of coloured pencils. The colour range includes bright primaries, subtle earth colours and pale tones.

COLOUR RANGES

There is no single system of naming or numbering pastel colours that would enable direct comparison between brands. The larger ranges of soft pastels, especially those that offer several different tints and shades of the major hues, are usually identified by colour names and numbers. The best way to judge the colours you need is to look at the actual pastels; most are sold singly as well as in boxed sets and are displayed in a way that enables you to compare colours. The texture of

the pastel can be an important influence on the effect of the colour, and charts that use printers' colours to identify the range cannot always show the true qualities.

When you start to handle the pastels you may find that there is a difference between the colour of a stick and the colour it produces when applied to your painting surface. Because of the composition of soft and hard pastels, dark colours particularly may change, coming up lighter on the paper. This is also affected importantly by the type of ground you choose to use, with regard to both its colour and texture; it may be helpful to make up your own colour charts showing the effects of your pastel palette on particular types of paper.

The degree of light-fastness of the colours in a pastel range naturally varies between different pigments, but the variation is relatively insignificant for practical purposes. Not all manufacturers provide a scale of light-fastness, but in artists' quality brands every effort is made to select pigments that will ensure true and lasting colours.

Colour sets
Pastel artists may build up a stock of literally hundreds of colours, though a single painting may utilize only a few. To facilitate selection, it helps to keep the similar hues arranged in sets. Soft pastel sticks break easily in the course of work, and are often broken deliberately to control the width of the stroke. All the smaller pieces are usable and worth preserving

PAPERS AND GROUNDS

It is a well-established tradition to apply soft pastels to a coloured ground, often paper of a firm quality with a pronounced grain providing surface tooth, but various types of board are also used. A distinct degree of texture is required to grip the loose pastel colour. In order to allow a build-up of layers developing form and detail in a composition, it is important that the pastel does not fill the tooth of the paper immediately; once the grain is lost, the pastel sticks begin to slide on the surface, rather than deposit colour easily. So the colour of the ground often shows through, and can make an important contribution to the overall picture.

Some types of coloured papers and boards are made specially for pastel work. Many artists prefer to use muted colours – greys, beiges and soft blue, green and sandy shades – that have a subtle influence, but there are also stronger paper colours, such as black, deep maroon and ultramarine, which can have a dramatic effect. The base colour may be chosen to correspond to something in the picture – green for landscape, for example, blue for marine subjects, sand and beige for sunlit townscapes; or it may be selected as a deliberate counterpoint to the colours that will be applied – a cool grey-blue to underlie hot oranges and yellows, a warm red-brown or ochre to send up the pitch of bright greens and blues.

The texture of the ground varies from evenly pitted and woven surfaces evolved from particular ways of finishing paper sheets, to the more random, rough and corrugated finishes of ordinary cardboard and packing boards. Some types of pastel paper are available mounted on

board, combining the particular surface effect with a more resistant weight and thickness. Heavily textured surfaces used for pastel work include abrasive finishes such as those of pumice, sand or glasspaper, which grip the colour very firmly and allow a dense build-up because it is not easy to fill the grain. On these papers an artist can achieve chunky impasto effects or solid masses of blended colour. There are softer textures, too, in velour paper, which has a gentle napped surface, and cork-coated paper, which is variable and giving. In fact, pastels can be applied to almost any surface, and one of the pleasures of the medium is choosing and exploiting particular qualities.

Abrasive papers
This detail of a soft pastel painting on glasspaper shows clearly the 'bite' of the pastel stroke on the gritty tooth of the surface. The warm brown colouring that is the natural finish of the paper is used as a positive element of the painter's palette

Coloured papers
The grain of pastel paper breaks up the applied colour, so that the colour of the ground shows through. Sometimes it is deliberately left bare to enhance contrasts. Here the subtle ground colour gives intensity to the hue, texture and edge quality of the red pastel strokes

Underpainting

Several of the masterclass artists use the technique of underpainting in watercolour, oil or acrylic to set a key for the pastel work and provide strong textural qualities.

For her painting Garden Tea, *Sally Strand put down a strong abstract pattern of light and dark shapes with acrylic paint* (TOP), *using colours that would contrast with and intensify the overlaid pastel hues and tones. The watercolour paper has a definite grain and the painting consists of free, loose brush strokes. In the finished work* (RIGHT), *these underlying textures break through the pastel, creating a very rich and complex interaction of surface detail* (BELOW)

An alternative is to lay a ground specially devised in relation to the style and subject of the composition. Pastels can be worked over various types of paint – oil, acrylic, water-colour and gouache – provided the paint layer does not smooth out the paper's texture, or, alternatively, creates its own. This enables the artist to 'custom build' not only the surface qualities of the ground, but also the appropriate colouring.

The above details apply to all types of dry or chalky pastels in which the colours are more or less opaque. Oil pastels are rather different, because of the moistness and greater translucency of the colours. As oil pastel strokes tend to blend and mesh quite fluidly, it may be preferable to work on a white ground that transmits some brilliance through the applied colours, as in painting. Good-quality water-colour and pastel papers, art boards and canvas boards are all suitable.

▶ Underpainting in watercolour
John Blockley's Venice Backwater *shows a very integrated use of watercolour underpainting to key the composition, using a technique that allows a strong random element (see pages 40–41). In some parts of the image the pastel work is very similar in hue and tone to the painted colour, so the shifts of light and texture in the image can tell very subtly*

TECHNIQUES

Pastels are unique in the way they combine the properties of drawing and painting media, enabling the artist to have such direct contact with the colours and to move very quickly and instinctively between the variations of line and mass in a composition. The marks you can make are infinitely variable, but the basic principle is very simple – it is mainly a matter of what area of the pastel makes contact with the surface, and how much pressure is applied.

HANDLING PASTELS

There are three important surfaces on a pastel stick: the tip, which provides a sharp line quality when handled decisively but also softens into thicker, grainy strokes; the side, which quickly wears down flatly so that it is possible to 'paint' with broad, sweeping strokes; and the long edge created by this wearing down, which with a little angled pressure can be made to form line and edge qualities quite different from those produced by working directly with the pastel tip.

With practice, the different ways of manipulating the pastel – switching from tip to side and varying the pressure – become second nature. Putting them to use effectively depends on gaining experience in

Using the pastel tip
The naturally linear emphasis of the pastel tip can be used for line qualities that vary from fragile traces to slashing scribbles. Shortening the marks into rough dashes and dots creates interesting textural variations and colour accenting

Side strokes
Using the long side of the pastel resembles painting with a broad brush. The colour can be swept in as grainy 'washes', but variations of angle and the pressure applied to the edge of the pastel length also bring out a clear sense of contour

observing your subject, and relating the movements of the pastel directly to the observed forms and textures. Beyond this lies the acquired confidence in the medium that enables an artist to experiment with techniques, and try a bold, unexpected move that may turn out to be the masterstroke.

BUILDING UP A SURFACE

The richness and variety of the pastel work demonstrated by the masterclass artists shows immediately that there is no single 'correct' route to a successful result. The most fascinating thing is that they all use pastels in different ways, and all equally achieve a special impact.

There are some interesting basic principles that can be drawn from the examples of these artists. The nature of the medium encourages a loose style of working initially, finding the general shapes and placing the tones and colours to establish the composition. The quality of the marks, however, can vary greatly – broad colour areas can be swept in with gentle side strokes, for example, or scribbled actively with the pastel tip. It is usually important to keep the surface textures light and open in the early stages, to avoid filling the ground texture and to leave all options open for layering and intensifying the colours.

Layers are built up either by overlaying side strokes to 'fatten' the surface colours or by continuing to overwork linear techniques, hatching and meshing the lines to increase the density of texture. In fact, any active surface will probably show a combination of both methods. Several of the masterclass artists pointed out that one of the vital aspects of technique is to be generous with

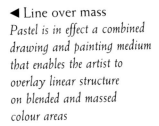

▶ Textural depth
A very rich and exciting surface is achieved through the combined techniques of blocking in solid colour areas with side strokes and drawing into shapes with the pastel tip. Linear contours and hatched or scribbled textures enhance the sense of pictorial depth

◀ Line over mass
Pastel is in effect a combined drawing and painting medium that enables the artist to overlay linear structure on blended and massed colour areas

Blending
Blending is often unnecessary, but with careful technique it can be a powerful feature of a composition. Geoff Marsters' method of rubbing soft pastel layers into the abrasive texture of pumice paper creates very subtle, singing blends, and he then reworks the blended areas to bring back the freshness of visible strokes (see page 92)

your materials. A delicious effect has no chance to develop if there is scarcely any colour on the paper.

Interestingly, few of the artists featured spend time on blending the colours physically by rubbing the surface and stroking the colours together with fingers or a rag. Blended effects are often apparent, but they develop incidentally, as the

15

build-up of overlaid strokes gradually coalesces. Actual blending techniques need to be used sparingly and with definite purpose, as they can muddy the colours and deaden the active surface qualities of soft pastel.

This illustrates an important quality of pastel work: seen close to, the uniformity of the surface breaks up. What appears 'realistic' from any distance – an object, portrait or landscape view – scatters into a mass of strokes, drifts and tiny points of colour once you look into it closely. A highly descriptive image can be composed of a surprisingly rough network of individual marks. It is important, then, to stand back from the work frequently and to gauge the pictorial effects that are emerging. This is probably true with any medium, but in pastel the abstract qualities of the marks are particularly significant to the final effect.

A problem that afflicts amateur and experienced artists alike is what to do with a passage that is working well, when the whole piece is not coming together satisfactorily. The seductive textures and colours of pastels mean that, even by chance, you may create a very beautiful effect at an early stage. However, the effort required to isolate and preserve this precious fragment can inhibit you from pushing the rest of the picture as far as it will go. Sometimes it is necessary to sacrifice what seems to be the best part of the work in order to progress the whole.

MIXING MEDIA

Richness and variation in the surface effects of an image are an important aspect of contemporary art. The characteristic marks and textures of the chosen medium are directly

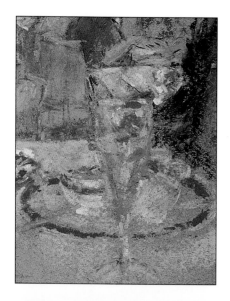

Broken colour
A broken surface is a typical feature of pastel work, the textural variations being a matter of degree. Each artist exploits this characteristic of the medium in a different way, but it is important to realize that clear forms and structures emerge from often very ragged and abstract patterns of pastel marks. This is demonstrated in a comparison of detailed areas from works by Diana Armfield (LEFT) *and Margaret Glass* (BELOW LEFT)

▼ Mixing pastel types
Integrating the textures of different pastels increases the artist's range of expression. In the early stages of this portrait, Tom Coates used hard pastel together with soft, both to point up the facial features and, as shown here, to pull together the softer strokes by hatching quickly and lightly across the surface

related to particular features of the subject portrayed, but also have a vitality of their own. Mixed-media techniques are now frequently used to exploit the different qualities of materials which can be combined sympathetically. The variations of technique and surface effect that mixed media provide may bring out specific attributes of the subject, help to create a mood, or give the artist a new way in to the composition.

Mixing different types of pastels is one example of this approach. There is an obvious logic to combining hard pastel or pastel pencil with soft

Charcoal and pastel
The slightly looser texture of charcoal makes it a good complement to soft pastel. Diana Constance used it here to establish a powerful drawing with strong darks into which she could float the powdery pastel colour

pastel – the media are closely related and the textural variations are mainly a matter of degree. A hard pastel or pencil can simply be easier to handle than a soft stick when you are dealing with fine detail or sharp contours. The combination of soft pastel and oil pastel, however, sets up a more complex interaction of textures. Oil sticks can be laid over the powdery colour of soft pastel and their lushness and moisture produces a rich glaze that contrasts with the opaque, matt colours; but when soft pastel is laid over oil, there is a 'resist' effect where the chalky texture adheres unevenly to the moist surface. This produces rich, irregular textures characteristically different from the broken colour effects of a single medium.

A work in soft pastel can be given a strong graphic framework by laying the colours over a drawing in charcoal or ink. Charcoal has a lighter, grittier quality than soft pastel, but its heavy blacks underpin the colour work dramatically. The fluid lines of an ink drawing make a dynamic contrast to the grainy textures of pastel. The strength of an underdrawing in black makes a bold

effect, but because soft pastel can be built up opaquely and has a giving texture, the pastel work can easily modify the original composition where required.

PASTEL AND PAINT

As already described, various kinds of paint are frequently used to form the ground for pastel work. Sometimes paint is applied simply to obtain an overall background of colour and texture of a kind not available from coloured papers. More often, the paint makes an active contribution based on the particular properties of the medium. Oils and acrylics, for example, give weight to the underpainting and influence the density of the textures. The translucence of watercolour establishes brilliant lights and colours in the composition which can be picked up and enhanced by the pastel overlays. It is also possible to rework paint over the pastel colours in a limited way, to revise parts of the image or develop detail; this needs a careful approach, as the paint does take up loose pastel dust.

Pastel over oil paint
A combination of media can help to set the mood of the subject, as well as contribute particular qualities of colour and texture. In this small painting, Approaching Dusk, *Debra Manifold applied an underpainting in oil to suggest the heavy, damp atmosphere of the winter landscape. Its weight and density enliven the impact of cold, sharp colours overlaid*

17

Watercolour and pastel
This is a wonderful combination of media for atmospheric subjects, when the artist can take advantage of watercolour's fluid, translucent quality and marry it with the grainy substantiality of opaque pastel colour.
   In Mountain Landscape (LEFT), *Diana Constance drew with the pastel over broad washes of watercolour, using the dry medium to strengthen colours and surface planes. In* Stormy Landscape (BELOW) *the pastel is more closely integrated with the paint: where the powdery colour was actually wetted, it was stirred into moody drifts and swirls*

Usually, a painted ground is allowed to dry almost completely, so the pastel can be woven over it without actually meshing the textures. But soft pastel can also be laid on a damp ground where the colour dissolves into a sort of paste. This creates flat, opaque colour areas or builds a rich impasto texture, depending on the weight and activity of the pastel strokes.

An alternative wet-and-dry technique is to use an appropriate solvent to spread the pastel colour, applied with a rag or brush. Soft

Wet-and-dry technique
In the foreground of this self-portrait you can see gentle brush strokes. Ken Paine has wetted the paper and spread the soft pastel colour on the damp surface. This technique creates a lyrical effect that benefits here from the mood of the monochrome treatment. It is a variation of line and wash drawing, with dry pastel strokes subtly strengthening the detail after the watery colour has dried

▼ Oil pastel and solvent
Oil pastel rubbed in places with turpentine obtains smoother qualities of colour and texture. The oil medium is combined here with soft pastel drawing

pastel can be wetted with clean water, for example, and spread into soft washes or fluidly brushed strokes. Turpentine is used to soften and blend oil pastel, making translucent veils of colour; this is also a method for disguising errors, removing the thickness of the pastel strokes and most of the colour so that the surface can be reworked.

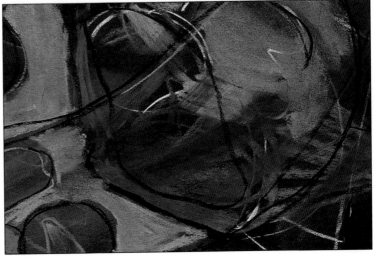

INTERPRETING THE SUBJECT

Techniques are not tricks to be learned independently; they arise naturally out of the effort to depict something expressively. There are actualities in the subject that show you where to block in extensive areas of colour and tone, where to harden a contour to form an edge, and where to place tiny accents of colour and highlights that bring the picture alive. While it may be interesting, and initially useful, just to play with the pastels and get the feel of them in your hand and on the paper, it is through interpreting real visual sensations that your technique is refined.

OBSERVATION AND SELECTION

The basic 'building blocks' of composition are shapes, tones and colours. Several of the masterclass artists stress searching for the fundamental structure of their subject, getting the relationship of the larger shapes in place before turning attention to the detail. This contradicts an almost instinctive desire to grapple directly with the attractive, impactful areas that first drew you to the subject. But the ability to break down the information, identify which elements of the subject make the most essential contribution and select what really counts towards building the image – this is the experienced artist's most important skill. It always underlies the physical skills of managing materials and techniques that are acquired through practice.

The masterclasses explain these connections clearly in terms of each individual artist's work; the particular sights and events that fire their enthusiasm for image-making feed into the techniques that they use to convey the ideas, and vice versa. In this section, however, the actual marks that they make to interpret certain subjects are for the moment studied separately, to extract some useful detail on how they have made the materials work for specific purposes.

Portraits

In portraiture, the artist must define what makes the likeness of the sitter and that direct response to the subject's characteristic features may suggest the technical approach.

Ken Paine uses the full strength of his colours and tones to model the heavily sculpted features of a middle-aged man (TOP), layering the soft pastel into variable textures. The blacks are relatively lightly glazed — you can see the paper grain through them — and Ken relies on the innate density of the colour to emphasize the hard shadows where the flesh folds in around eyes and nose. By contrast, he applies the pale and brilliant colours thickly to intensify the lights.

The female portrait by Tom Coates (RIGHT) is appropriately more delicate in tone and texture. The linear qualities of soft and hard pastels are exploited to weave a fabric of subtle nuances. The surface becomes progressively more integrated where hard pastel marks mesh into the softer textures and wrap the colours around the form. In places he accentuates the contours of the face, and points up the features with tiny, decisive touches of extreme tonal contrast

Figures

The overall shape and posture of a figure can be more crucial to recognition than the person's facial features. In these examples, it is not important for the viewer to be able to identify the subject, as may be the case in a portrait, but the artists have put recognizably real people before us by conveying very precisely the shapes of the bodies and their balances of weight and motion. The images have this in common despite the very different techniques.

Diana Constance uses rich tonal massing and creates tangible contours etched into the depth of the colours (TOP LEFT). Diana Armfield conjures the weight of her figures out of a seemingly fragile, broken surface of soft pastel (TOP RIGHT). The sense of form is anchored by brief linear emphases. Sally Strand's singing colours and active strokes build a solid figure out of pure light, by careful attention to the shifts and contrasts of the tonal values (BELOW)

Trees

This is a large subject with infinite possible variations of colour and texture. The artists take up the visual cues of the actual shapes and colours of the trees, the mood of the setting and the way the light falls in front of or behind the tree masses.

In these examples, both John Blockley and Debra Manifold deal with stark tree trunks as negative shapes standing out strongly against their background. John builds brilliant soft pastel colour over a black-painted ground, allowing the forms of trunks and branches to shape themselves against the light (TOP). *Debra's ghostly white trees shimmer amid warm autumnal colours, with soft and hard pastel worked over a watercolour base* (BELOW LEFT). *In the soft pastel painting by Geoff Marsters, the shapes are simplified and given form and density with a heavy massing of strokes in close harmony* (BELOW RIGHT). *The lights and colours evoke the serene, quiet mood of the secluded setting*

Flowers

The first striking impression of flowers is often the pure, bright colours, so it is almost irresistible to match this with one of the most important properties of pastels — the richness and variety of the colour range.

In Summer Glory *Frances Treanor applies bold strokes to the intricate shapes and patterns of massed flowers, letting each hue and tone have its most scintillating value* (OPPOSITE). *John Blockley's combination of watercolour and pastel in* Flower Group *weaves the colours into complex textures* (RIGHT). *Both paintings have an abstract quality in the way they deal with shapes and forms. Frances goes for strong edge qualities and tangled rhythms; John allows the forms to merge more fluidly but pulls out startling, spiky shapes that gain impact from the contrast. In Diana Armfield's* Sunflowers *the flowers emerge simply and dazzlingly from their field of soft blue-greens* (BELOW RIGHT). *A busy mass of loose, gentle strokes coalesces into flowers and background*

Water

The precise visual details of moving water are difficult to analyse. The colours seem to come from within, and are constantly changing.

Margaret Glass uses surprisingly free, loose strokes to achieve a very effective impression. From a little distance, the strokes form a coherent surface that suggests the reflective quality of water broken up in the wake of a fast-moving boat (TOP). In the second example (CENTRE), the greater swell of the waves is conveyed through a well-defined pattern of dark and mid-tones, topped with bright white foam which is lit with clear yellow. In still water the surface is all reflected colour (BELOW). Here again, Margaret studies the tonal patterns carefully and renders the effect of hard-edged shapes in a restricted colour range. Notice, too, how the direction of the strokes indicates both the depth – vertical strokes – and the glassy stillness – horizontals – of the water

Light

Many artists whose primary interest is painting light effects choose pastel as a particularly sympathetic medium for its intensity of colour. Typically, the pastel colours glow on the surface. But in soft pastel, especially, it can be difficult to get an intensity of dark tones; strong light effects are often orchestrated by subtle colour interactions rather than straight tonal oppositions.

Diana Armfield uses a range of pale, clean tints to find the fresh quality of cool daylight among a network of intricate shapes (TOP). Sally Strand also deals with the pattern of shapes created by the light that models form and depth, defining it strongly through the interplay of warm and cool colours (BELOW)

MASTERCLASS
with Diana Armfield

Diana Armfield's pastels reveal stored memories of the world around her: the light and colour of a scene; the particular structures and spaces of an interior or exterior view; the people who come and go within a setting; and the telling, sometimes tiny details that have caught her eye. The process of building up the pastel colour creates an image that at first sight gives a vivid glimpse of the original impression, then gradually unfolds further layers of information through the artist's thoughtful management of composition and technique.

This information is acquired by drawing: by watching and absorbing subjects and recording them in sketches and studies. Diana seldom uses photographic reference for her work, although she takes pleasure in photographs in the ordinary way, as mementoes of personal experiences. But as an artist, she feels that photographs obliterate rather than enhance the visual memories; the camera is selective, but it does not select the same things that she would choose to focus on. The process of drawing, however, allows time for the subject 'to go into you and become part of you' – she describes this as a kind of nourishment. If you sit and draw for an hour or more, you can take in the sights, smells and atmosphere, and 'observation becomes more acute. You come away with an idea, which the drawing will have in it, and when you look at the drawing that idea comes back, and it's not superseded by anything else.'

▶ The Plaza Tearoom
190×180 mm ($7\frac{1}{2}×7$ in)
This painting reflects Diana's delight in re-creating the detail of an opulent setting with the rich tones and hues of soft pastel. She is fascinated with the patterning of colours and shapes, both in surface patterns such as the carpet and tapestry chair-backs, and in the structure of the room with its arches, elaborate lamps and network of tables and chairs.

The seated woman in the foreground should be a dominant feature, but is deliberately played down. Edge qualities are important: the woman in the hat is outlined on one side by the more intense tones of the second figure; below, her hands and arms merge gently into the colours of the table setting. Similarly, there are varied emphases in the shapes and contours describing the space and furnishings of the room that subtly reorganize the viewer's sense of space and form as the eye moves across the picture surface

MATERIALS AND METHODS

Diana uses soft graphite pencils, 4B or 5B, for her sketchbook drawings, describing the scene in line and tone and sometimes adding written notes that record particular qualities of light and colour. She does not work in pastels on the spot: the sketches may later be interpreted in oil paint, watercolour or pastel, perhaps in more than one medium, and it is often obvious to her which she will eventually choose. It may be a matter of weeks or months before she returns to a sketch to develop the subject in pastel – another reason why it is important for her to absorb the scene so fully while she is drawing at the location.

On some occasions, when she is sure the subject lends itself to pastel, she draws direct on pastel paper using soft, chalky pencils, choosing

QE II

205×215 mm $\left(8 \times 8\frac{1}{2} in\right)$
The sketch from which the pastel was derived (ABOVE), developed freely across facing pages of a sketchbook, is more a reminder of the atmosphere and detail than a positive framework for the drawing. The composition (RIGHT) has been considerably adapted, with Diana using her memories of the scene and experience of re-creating her visual impressions to expand and elaborate the picture. It has a beautiful sense of the daylight under partial shade, and the relaxed enjoyment of such a situation

In the Gallery, Art
Institute of Chicago
180×215 mm (7×8½ in)
*The subtle tone of the cool
grey paper is used extensively
to make the colours sing,
particularly the warm pinks
and reds. Getting the right
impression for the paintings on
the wall was an interesting
problem. The large picture on
the right was originally going
to be the brightest area of the
composition, but Diana
realized this would make it
appear to be a window, as
light outdoors is always
stronger than in an interior.
She adjusted the key of that
area, revising the distribution
of tones overall*

from a range of browns varying between light and dark tones. In this way the drawing, which is mainly linear, becomes the underlayer for the pastel. These coloured pencils have no greasy content at all, so it is easy to rub away the lines to correct or modify the drawing. Diana uses old bristle brushes to soften edges and lift or erase the chalk where necessary.

The paper is usually a firm pastel paper, which has a rough, pitted grain on one side and a smoother, toothed surface on the other. Diana prefers to use the smoother side, finding the heavy grain too mechanical in texture.

The choice of paper colour depends on the mood and tonality of the subject. She selects a warm, honey-coloured ground or a subtle, blue-grey mid-tone, nothing very dark or very light. The warm colour is intended either to complement warm hues in the pastel painting, or to interact with cool colours and make them sing out. On a warm ground a clear blue sky, for example, is very radiant, whereas on blue-grey paper it loses that brilliance. But Diana enjoys the 'lighthearted' tone of the blue-grey, particularly for a subject that has an airy quality.

She likes to allow the colour of the paper to show through the areas of pastel, and sometimes it will act as one of the key colours in the painting – such as a warm buff colour standing for the colour of a wall in a townscape. She stresses that the applied colour needs to 'breathe', and one way of achieving this is to avoid covering the paper solidly with pastel: allowing the ground to show through maintains the sparkle and illumination of the picture.

A useful point Diana makes about choosing paper is to consider positively what the size and proportion

Buffet Lunch on the
QE II
The sketch of this subject was drawn on pastel paper with the intention of applying colour over the drawing. It became very detailed, and Diana decided to expand the composition, so she worked the finished pastel separately

of the work should be, as well as the texture and colour of the ground. The picture should fit the scale of the idea; the size of the image should not be determined by the dimensions of the paper.

CONTROLLING THE COLOUR

Diana describes her ideal way of achieving a pastel painting as beginning with an exquisite suggestion of the drawing and then just drifting the pastel into it in the right places – a 'dialogue between the drawing and the pastel, with nothing over-worked'. However, with typical practicality, she notes that this rarely happens so effortlessly, and she does rely on being able to remove the colour with a soft eraser. The paper she uses can take a certain amount of erasure and still allow the overlaid strokes to appear fresh. Once this kind of reworking has occurred and the 'drifted' quality is lost, she recommends going all out to build up the richness of the painting.

As a practised pastellist, Diana has a vast range of pastels of varying properties and colours. She selects as many as she feels she needs for the subject, but reckons that for any one painting her palette might consist of just a dozen or so pastel sticks. She keeps these together in her hand, or in a box lid, while working and prefers to manipulate this small selection, rather than continually look for another and another colour. Still, she says, there are times when she finds herself 'searching for an ideal fragment buried among a host of other pastel pieces'.

FIXING PASTELS

Diana takes a practical approach to using fixative. She prefers to avoid it, as it can bring down the key of a painting appreciably, but will fix a work that has to travel soon after it is completed, for example, or one that is generally dark-toned and may even gain in richness as a result. When she has applied fixative, she

reworks the pale tones to bring up the lights, as the brighter pastel colours are more likely to be dulled by fixing. Her usual method is to allow the finished pastel to lie on a shelf with air circulating freely around it, where it may stay for about a month while a frame is being made. During this time, she believes, the humidity of the room helps to set the colour. She has encountered problems with chalky residue falling from the surface only when a work has been framed and transported immediately after it is finished. Otherwise, she finds that fixing her work is mostly unnecessary.

Buffet Lunch on the QE II

195×260 mm $\left(7\frac{3}{4}×10\frac{1}{4}\ in\right)$

In this interior view of the ocean liner, the dazzling cool light from the sea is strongly conveyed through the window panels of clear pale blue, made brilliant and opaque by the relative thickness of the pastel application. Their large, regular shapes offset the detail and activity within the buffet room, where the pastel colour has the gentle 'drifted' quality that Diana enjoys. The broad lighting from the back is picked up again in the tiny touches of bright colour and highlighting on the foreground figures, which sparkle out of the deeper, more sombre tones

Volterra

210×165 mm ($8\frac{1}{4}×6\frac{1}{2}$ in)

The townscape of Volterra contrasts with the view of Orvieto (opposite), both in the character of the place itself and the pictorial arrangement. It is a more austere town, with narrow streets that fall into heavy shadow. Here a brilliant patch of light breaking through unexpectedly is placed in the middle ground of the painting. The organization of the composition reflects the sense of enclosure, but its movement comes towards you, from the lit tower at the back through the shaft of sunlight to the shadowy column of intriguing shapes in the left foreground; whereas in Orvieto the open space of the foreground leads away into the dark

COMPOSITION

Composing the picture is not one discrete stage of the work, after which there is an image in the mind's eye that can be transferred to the paper. It is a continual process that begins in the sketches and can go on right to the point where the finished pastel is ready for framing.

In her drawings Diana may have a framework, such as the architecture of a street or interior, on which she notes the changing rhythms, primarily of people entering and leaving the scene, but also of the counterpoint of light and shadow, and incidental details of the permanent setting that become gradually more evident.

When it comes to developing the pastel work, Diana begins with the drawing but stresses that she uses the colours to reinterpret the subject, playing naturally against the lines – 'over, up and within'. She may begin with an idea of certain effects that she wishes to achieve. In *Orvieto*, for example, while making the sketch, she placed the solid vertical plane of the church to the right and looked for a general tonal balance in which there would be more dark

Orvieto

210 × 150 mm (8¼ × 6 in)
*The finished pastel shows how
the original drawing has been
revised. The framework is the
same but the perspective is
slightly pulled back, extending
the view and deepening the
foreground. Diana deliberately
enlarged the closest figures, and
their implied movement from
left to right contrasts with the
other subjects' motion away
from the viewer. Experimenting
with an unfamiliar paper
and a brush-pen for the
underdrawing, Diana felt that
the pen's even flow of ink
created a too-consistent line
quality. The subsequent pastel
work obliterated much of it,
although the crisp ink line is
still visible in the foreground
figures and in the tower
at the back.*

*The scene conveys the
warm light of late afternoon,
when the pattern of shadows
'makes everything composable'.*

*The small patch of blue sky
sings out intensely against the
sandy brown paper, which
also enhances the blue, violet
and neutral grey shadows.
Much of the activity resides in
the figures, but the overall
balance of the composition is
strengthened by small touches
such as the white noticeboard,
with its contrasting dark edge,
on the pink church wall*

35

than light. In the pastel, the figures could then emerge in counterpoint to their background tones; but the precise interactions of colour and shape, and even the actual scale of important elements, could develop quite freely from the progress of the work itself.

For practical reasons, she will usually start at the top of the picture and work down, to avoid smudging colours and details as they are laid in. Therefore, the shape and colour of the sky may form the key for the composition. As the overall picture develops, however, she works to and fro across the surface, building the tones and making those adjustments and small touches that increase the vitality of the image. Where there is a lot of complex detail in the foreground, as in the prominent still-life element of *Fortnum's*, this naturally comes last, although there will have been a suggestion of it from the beginning.

In reference to the initial drawing, Diana describes holding up her hands to make a frame for the view, deciding how much of it she will include. This decision can be altered when reworking the scene for the pastel, but she may also adjust the proportions again at a later stage, extending the image or cropping out an existing part. The composition need not be finalized until the mount goes on the picture.

PICTORIAL QUALITIES

An interesting, and perhaps unexpected, piece of advice from Diana on developing a pastel is to avoid worrying about how to get it to 'look like' the original subject. Because the colour work relates directly to the drawing, it is tempting to be too explicit, with the result that an illustrative feel can occur. To prevent this Diana consciously deals with the abstract elements of the composition – rhythms, directions, edge qualities, tone and colour. 'Looking like', she says, is a by-product of

▶ Nora's Fish Café
205 × 215 mm (8 × 8½ in)
Diana's particular interest in this subject was at first the elaborate lamps with their shell-shaped shades and brilliant colours. But as she worked on the drawing and became more involved with the figures, she realized it was impossible to focus so much detail in one image. Her interest in the individual characters, the pattern of shapes in the diners' hats and the subtle mixture of colour values led her to abandon any attempt to make the lamps a special feature. This is a useful illustration of the way a composition does not always turn out as the artist expects, once the process of selecting and organizing the varied elements has begun. The pastel is applied, in this case, over the actual drawing Diana made at the café

◀ Fortnum's
150 × 190 mm (6 × 7½ in)
This is an interesting example of the way Diana uses the viewer's natural attraction to human subjects to develop an unusual perspective. There is a kind of horizontal layering, with the figures pushed well back, enabling the artist to make a beautifully abstract play of colour and light on the large-scale still-life element in the immediate foreground. The tonal range is reversed from what might be expected, with the stronger contrasts in the background, but the larger shapes and glittering detail in the foreground create a balance

getting all these things right. The two layers of the picture move along together: 'the abstract should be drawn from the scene, and the scene should be held in the abstract life'. One of the formal aspects that she orchestrates very effectively is the interplay between simplicity and complexity, such as an area of solid colour played off against an intricate, rich pattern. She also looks for lively contrasts of colour and tone.

An important quality is what Diana calls 'lost and foundness', the unfolding of the image so that different elements strike the viewer at different times. She feels it is quite acceptable not to work all areas of the pastel to the same pitch, so that some parts become explicit, others remain veiled or merely suggested. It can be difficult, she adds, to carry this through, for whatever part of the image you are working on at the moment tends to be the most important in your mind.

Figures feature prominently in many of Diana's compositions, and she makes the useful point that human subjects always attract attention and therefore it is not necessary always to feature them in a dominant position. There are particularly interesting examples of the way she deals with this in *Fortnum's* and *The Plaza Tearoom*. It is also part of allowing the components of the image to be discovered – the idea of 'playing with what tells, and what tells later'.

MASTERCLASS
with John Blockley

The colour in John Blockley's paintings creates structure, form and mood. John takes advantage of the full spectrum of the pastel palette, handling the most vibrant hues with confidence and often applying them to large areas of a painting, but equally in command of its subtler ranges – clean greys, soft ochres and deep, shadowy purples, browns and blues that contribute to the atmosphere of landscape and interior subjects. The impression of the colour mood is often very strong, but many complex influences emerge, derived both from the mixing of colours on the surface and from the varied character of the pastel marks.

One of the important decisions in pastel painting is choosing the right surface to work on – one that contributes to the visual qualities of the rendering and complements the artist's techniques of applying and building up the pastel. John Blockley has developed a method of preparing a ground for his work which provides a surface that is active and contributory right from the start, a unique entry to the individual subject.

▶ Lakeside Trees
1070×790 mm (42×31 in)
The strong network of trunks and branches was formed by dealing directly with the negative shapes – the spaces between the trees. The pastel is applied to a dense black ground of acrylic paint, so that the darkest tones are represented by untouched areas of the board. The actual base is a mount board which has a slight ripple in the surface, an effect transmitted in the shimmer of the stroked-on colour where the underlayers break through. In places the pastel is pressed down more heavily to fill the surface, so that the colours become intense and quite opaque.

The shapes within the trees suggested the shape and scale of the marks applied to the lower section of the picture. At first these were interesting echoes of the tree structures, but they evolved into the effect of a sparkling reflection on the water

THE UNDERPAINTING

Rather than choose a coloured pastel paper intended either to key in or offset the pastel colours, John makes a loosely washed painting on white watercolour paper. This gives him a variable ground with many nuances of shape, texture, tone and colour directly related to features of the actual landscape or still life, say, that is his subject.

John prefers to use lightweight paper with a hot-pressed surface finish, so that there is minimal texture. His pastel techniques create very complex textures and he does not want these to be dictated by the paper grain. He makes the underpainting in watercolour, laid in very freely, allowing colours to run together in places and letting certain parts dry out completely to harden the shapes and edges. Then he plunges the whole sheet into a bath of water and lets the still-wet colour wash off. This retrieves some of the whites, where paint which is lightly brushed and still damp disappears completely; modifies the tones and hues; and sharpens the contrast of defined shapes and atmospheric

Demolition
330×225 mm (13×9 in)
The washed-out, dusky pink of the watercolour base is still very visible in the foreground of this painting, but John enjoyed introducing similarly muted pastel tints that create a necessary surface variation without interrupting the sweep of the larger shapes. The profile of the building was what first drew his attention, and he has sharply etched this against the background and sky by utilizing vibrant contrasts of colour and tone. The contours are sharpened delicately with hints of drawing in pastel pencil

G. John Blockley.

Welsh Cottages

330×305 mm (13×12 in)
The layering of the
composition pushes most of
the detail into the upper half
of the picture. The pattern
of interlocking planes that
constructs the cottages is very
loosely and subtly reprised in
the massing of broad strokes
forming the grassland spread
out below. This reverses the
typical device of placing the
areas of greatest complexity in
the foreground of a landscape
painting, with the definition of
form and detail usually shown
to diminish with increasing
distance from the viewer. Here,
however, the space of the
painting is restricted by the
vertical emphasis of the subject

textures. Washing out creates both positive and negative impressions: for example, in his flower paintings the water bath may rinse off particular shapes within the generalized mass of the flower arrangement.

The result is a first-stage painting that combines deliberation and accident, an image which has the essence of the subject in it but is still full of potential. John emphasizes that it is not a process of making a painting of the subject, then putting the pastel marks over it – the under-

painting is suggestive, not a blueprint for the finished work. The colours may relate directly to those seen – as in the dusky pinks and reds of *Demolition* – or they may be chosen to counterpoint in hue or tone the pastel colours that will subsequently be worked into various parts of the image – such as the warm but muted shades underlying the grassy foreground in *Welsh Cottages*, which give more vibrancy to the superimposed greens and blues.

This technique is applied to all sorts of subjects; because there are so many variable factors, it cannot become predictable. The approach is direct and informal – John even describes the effect he wants as 'uncouth'. He uses housepainter's brushes to apply the watercolour, 'sloshing it on' with a loose technique that both keeps the washes free and builds in touches of brushed texture here and there.

However, although this process provides an open but positive basis for the pastel work, John does not make it a strict formula for his initial approach. For *Lakeside Trees*, for example, he painted the mountboard support with opaque black acrylic. The very substance of the paint, as compared to the translucency and fluidity of watercolour, and the dramatic choice of the darkest of dark tones gave him a very different starting point. In typically informal style, the acrylic was applied with a 125 mm (5 in) decorator's brush with, as the artist says, 'no finesse about it'.

Connemara
560×760 mm (22×30 in)
There is a powerful attraction in the apparent bleakness of certain landscapes. The main mood of the piece is established by the cold silvery greys, but counterpointed by the gold-edged sliver of land in the middle ground. The contrast of hard and soft marks increases the surface interest of the broad expanses. Hatching is used as a literal element for describing the waterside reeds, which are lit at the tips with tiny glints of light, made by stabbing into the pastel colour with a blade

APPLYING THE PASTEL

Occasionally, John starts working with soft pastels while the under-painting is still damp, so that the powdery colour forms a sort of paste on the paper which dries with a velvety texture. This approach depends upon visual cues in the subject; he might use the technique where he wants relatively flat colour areas – the roofs in *Welsh Cottages*, for example, but not the foreground.

Otherwise, he begins to build up colour and texture using soft pastels once the underpainting has dried, working with the tip and side of the pastel stick and varying the directions of the strokes. He keeps the image very open initially, then takes up harder pastels and works into the soft layers, making criss-cross marks which are allowed to lift and drag the colours already applied. He creates a sort of mesh with the different kinds of strokes, concerned all the while to keep the texture active. He does not deliberately rub in the pastel, and if it incidentally becomes rubbed down by the movements of his hand, he goes back over the flattened area to rework the meshing of directional strokes.

John does not follow any particular colour sequence, but while applying one colour to part of the painting he may pause to pay particular attention to where else it might go, especially when it is a dominant hue. The work is an integrated process of putting the colour on, then breaking it down. The latter may occur through the crosshatching of hard pastel over soft, or John may break into the surface with a scalpel or razor blade, sometimes 'flicking through the layers' in a way that lifts out the pastel colour, to retrieve glimpses of the underpainting. He finds little trouble in keeping the colours clean and fresh, but may occasionally apply fixative to facilitate the layering of the textures.

FORM AND SPACE

The idea of making positive use of 'negative areas' of the composition is an important principle in John's work. Such areas may be the overall background surrounding the subject, or the shapes made in the spaces between objects. In flower or figure paintings, his usual method is to lay in the background first, allowing the main subject to emerge as a negative image. He says a typical problem for inexperienced painters is that they tend to work up the positive image in too much detail – for example, painting the flowers in an arrangement very carefully while ignoring their relation to the surround – so that the subject 'does not enter the background'. He also warns against dealing with one item at a time, when the whole image may fail to cohere. The key is to look for the overall pattern of shapes, to simplify the initial steps of the painting and identify the links and oppositions.

By working, as it were, from the outside in, John has a sense both of the active shapes and colours of the background and of the emerging shape of, say, a flower group. One advantage of this method is that, because the background is usually simpler than the central subject, you can establish its general composition quite quickly and get into a confident relationship with the painting before tackling the more complex detail. The principle does not apply only to flower paintings, or compositions that similarly have a clearly defined figure-ground relationship. The dramatic framework of *Lakeside Trees* was constructed by using the

▶ Flower Group
610×510 mm (24×20 in)
John's usual method when painting flowers is to lay in the background first, so that the shape of the arrangement is barely explained. He then works into the more complex detail of the flowers. Here he contrasts simple colour areas with vigorous hatched and crosshatched textures, putting the colours alongside one another, then slashing through them and breaking up the masses. At the same time he allows rhythmic links and repetitions to develop between the shapes

pastel to develop the shapes between the trunks and branches, allowing the strong black under-painting to force its way through on equal terms with the bright colours.

As work progresses on a painting, the textures of paint and pastel are gradually knitted together, as are the shapes and rhythms of the composition. John looks for balances and echoes – the massing of forms set against open expanses, individual shapes in the subject repeated as shadows of themselves or by chance connections. There is often one colour that has a strong presence, occurring in several related hues, tints and shades, balanced by bright accents of opposite colours or sudden tonal contrasts.

MEDIUM AND SUBJECT

John has worked with pastel ever since he began to take an interest in painting and drawing. He also paints in watercolour, the number of works in either medium about evenly divided within his annual output. He may at a given time be more interested in one than another, exploring its possibilities intensively for a period.

His landscapes demonstrate a keen sense of place. He has a particular feeling for the vigour of the countryside around his studio in the north of England, depicted in *Derbyshire Moors*, and its relation to the industrial settings of that region. But as the examples of his landscapes reproduced here show, the jumbled, informal architecture of a Welsh village, the moody enclosure of a Venetian canal (see page 12) or the bare, open spaces of the Irish coastline come equally vividly to life in his handling of pastel colour and texture. He rarely works outdoors on pastel paintings now, finding that sketchbook references are increasingly important.

Derbyshire Moors
760×810 mm (30×32 in)
The structure of this painting derives from a decision to divide the ground quite simply – one line straight down the middle, one running across – and then to make the configuration work. This John does by creating strong shapes and activating them with complex, atmospheric textures. The overall colour harmony is woven out of vivid pure hues and dramatic contrasts set against heavy neutral tones. This combination aptly reflects the rugged beauty of the spacious landscape laid out under a turbulent sky

The lively pencil sketch of Aran (above) was translated into colour with a combination of watercolour and pastel simply to investigate how it might work, and the spontaneity of the original is revitalized in the colour study.

In line with his informal approach to beginning a work, John is happy to treat it quite irreverently while it is in progress. He may be working on several subjects at once, and likes to leave the paintings lying around the studio casually, even on the floor, so that he may catch an unexpected glimpse that triggers some new development. With a lack of sentimentality that is almost disconcerting, he observes that when painting flowers he prefers them to be dead – or at a stage of dying where there is enough to remind him of what they were, but when the shapes and forms have developed an angularity and crispness that sharpens his rendering.

He will look for a subject that poses a new challenge, that presses him to find 'a means of definition'; or he may set himself a formal problem to be solved, such as the simple but severe vertical and horizontal divisions in *Derbyshire Moors*. There are different possibilities to explore for finding the way into a particular painting; in John's own words, 'We need to adjust our mental attitude to suit the nature of each work we undertake.'

Aran

330×305 mm (13×12 in)
The linear emphasis of this pastel and watercolour study relates directly to the on-the-spot pencil sketch (ABOVE LEFT) from which it is derived. It has the same vital, calligraphic contours, but the textural qualities are enhanced by the colour work. The heavy sky is an interesting factor, a sympathetic balance to the solid shapes and dark tonal key of the landscape detail; a pale sky would have dramatically thrown the foreground into relief

MASTERCLASS
with Tom Coates

Tom Coates takes a versatile approach to his materials and techniques. He has always used pastel, as well as working in oil paint and watercolour; the choice of medium and his method of handling it are a response to the situation in which he is working at a given time, and to the particular subject. His pastel techniques are firmly based in his drawing skills, and he enjoys the differences both of the varied kinds of marks that can be made and of the contrasting textures of soft and hard pastels. He employs the linear qualities of the medium very fully, sometimes using pastel purely for monochrome drawing or as a means of making location sketches in line and colour. But he also creates very complex and rich-textured images by using the variety of the pastel marks to layer a dense mesh of overlaid colours, building forms that have solidity and mass, alive with surface detail.

▶ Kimonos
1830 × 1220 mm (72 × 48 in)
The brilliance and luminosity of the kimonos come from both the selection of vibrant pastel hues and the active, varied handling of the medium as the strength of the drawing is built up on the black ground. This startling contrast of high-key colours on the darkest possible surface gives the artist instant feedback – 'you can see what you're doing right away'. The scale of the image was obtained by working on two large pieces of mount board joined together. Tom has created a beautiful rhythm by gradually increasing the complexity of the pastel work in certain areas, focusing the detail on the upper bodies and heads and illuminating them with the loose, broad pattern of very light tints behind

WORKING WITH THE SUBJECT

Tom has no set method or procedure: he engages with the mood of the moment. A lot of his work involves the human figure and he will not bring a preconceived idea to the approach. He studies the sitter and sees perhaps two or three different compositions that would express the pose; when he has chosen the viewpoint, he blocks in the pastel by drawing very rapidly, establishing the key shapes and colour values but keeping the surface loose and open. He describes the composition as having a 'chaotic' activity at this stage, in which there are many possibilities to be drawn out. Tom likes to hold this vigorous, suggestive impression for a while before he goes on to develop the drawing to a finish.

It is natural for him to work quickly and his observation of the subject is translated directly onto the working surface. When he is blocking in, he watches the model intently and lets his hand travel easily across the picture area, laying down loose colour and texture: 'It's nice to get the whole thing on rather than just a little area, because it's very easy suddenly to go too far.' As the image takes shape, he remains alert to the way a slight shift of emphasis in one area affects the whole.

In the course of developing the work, his approach tends to be practical rather than analytical. If he feels something isn't working, he quickly tries out a move that will change it – a different colour or different tension in the marks – and responds immediately to the new directions that offers. If the circumstances create particular pressures on his concentration, as when he is drawing in an outdoor location or demonstrating for an interested audience, he may

do some considered reworking when he returns to his studio to 'tidy up' and redefine the shapes. 'When I work on the spot, I just work. When I get back to the studio I can solve the problems, although, in fact, you're problem-solving all the time.'

Tom is also quick to pick up an opportunity for an exciting composition based on a momentary event. One such is recorded in his small pastel *Model Resting*, when a break in the life class took the model out of her formal pose as she accepted a cup of tea. Tom has used strong tones and colours dashed in quite loosely and freely to create an image with a relaxed, spontaneous mood; a tiny slice of life captured in just a few minutes' work. A similar mood in a quite different situation is expressed in his colour sketch of *The Ghats at Udaipur*, one of many drawings he made during a visit to India. Here the fragile line work rapidly traces the transient poses of

Model Resting
305 × 255 mm (12 × 10 in)
Working quickly on this small drawing to capture an incidental moment that created an intriguing composition, Tom blocked in the shapes broadly with grainy strokes, building up simple colour areas that depict the essence of the forms. He used rich, immediate hues and tones, looking for strong highlights and colour accents that enliven the picture

50

people going about their business at the water's edge. The limited palette conveys the bright light bathing the scene and the flickering colours of moving figures and reflections on the water.

MATERIALS AND TECHNIQUES

The physical properties of the materials are employed to good effect. Tom works on various types of paper and board; the colour and texture of the ground often contribute significantly to the finished drawing. He likes the coarseness and earthy colourings of ordinary cardboard and packing boards, uses coloured pastel papers and mount boards with even, strong tones, and for large-scale work often stretches up big pieces of heavy watercolour paper cut from

the roll. He enjoys working expansively – typically his pastel drawings are generously proportioned and he often does half- and full-length portraits at close to life size.

Tom mixes hard and soft pastels, choosing the size, texture and colour of each stick as appropriate to the particular marks he wishes to make. Large, very soft pastels are used on the tip and side for blocking in broad colour areas, and smaller sticks with a slightly more compact texture for refining the tones and shapes in the drawing. Tom takes advantage of the crisper line qualities of hard pastel to work into details, introduce points of tension, and bring together the textures of the looser marks. In particular, at certain times when he has built up a mass of overlaid soft pastel colours, he will lightly hatch all over the area with hard pastel to make the

The Ghats at Udaipur
510×760 mm (20×30 in)
This drawing combines the freshness of a rapid on-the-spot sketch with the conviction of a detailed, finished statement. The technique is quite sparing, but the information is enough to re-create a vivid feeling of the scene. Bright colour is used for vibrant accenting within a powerful tonal structure

◀ Young Student
560×405 mm (22×16 in)
Because the colours of pastel
are so obviously enticing, it is
not always fully explored as
a tonal drawing medium. This
kind of emphatically linear
drawing would also work in
pencil or charcoal, but the
properties of hard black pastel
contribute a dense but giving,
variable line quality that
encourages the bold
calligraphic treatment

▶ Woman with Dark
Hair
1015×810 mm (40×32 in)
Tom uses the tip and side of
the pastel sticks to block in
basic colour areas very
rapidly with a vigorous
scribbling motion (1). From
the beginning, he combines
hard and soft pastels to vary
the textures and tensions of the
drawing.

Initially, he develops the
contours and general pattern
of the shapes, still working
freely and selecting colours
that establish the overall key
of the palette (2).

He has already begun to
mix the colours on the face,
contrasting delicate, warm
flesh tints with cold blue
shadows. At the same time as
drawing into the face and hair
to develop the structure of the
portrait, he pays attention to
the way this is balanced by
the background and clothing,
so that no one area of the
image gets too far ahead of
another (3).

▲ 1

▲ 2

▼ 3

surface texture more cohesive and
draw up the colours from underneath, subtly adjusting the sense of
form. This technique works because
the hard edge of the stick disturbs
the softer colour in a controlled way
and does not lay down too much
colour of its own.

An interesting aspect of Tom's
work is the variety of textures he
achieves, both within a single work
and as applied to different subjects.
He is prepared to limit himself to the
graphic simplicity of using hard
black pastel alone in the drawing
Young Student, where strong, fluid
contours are woven through the vigorous shading and hatching that
model form and volume. He is
equally in command of the dense
colour layering that creates the
glowing light and fascinating texture

▲ 4   ▼ 5

▼ 6

▲ This detail shows how
loose hatching drawn across
the flesh tones with hard pastel
has lightly 'cut into' the mass
of softer colours and
emphasized the shadowing
around nose and chin by
letting hints of the underlying
colours come through

▼ 7

These broad shapes are
darkened at this stage, and
Tom flicks in an impression of
the detail – marks that convey
folds in the clothing and the
texture of the fabric (4).

He draws in a definite
shape for the hand, remarking
that the strong black contour
acts 'as a full stop' at the
bottom of the picture. At this
stage he is moving continually
between different areas of the
drawing, strengthening tones
and redefining the detail. Pale
tints on the face enhance the

luminosity of eyes and skin.
He tries a stronger colour for
the background (5).

This block of deep red
behind the head is used to key
an enrichment of tones and
colours within the figure (6).

In the final stage the deeper
hue is actively worked into the
whole background plane and
the contours of the figure are
drawn again in black line to
bring the shapes forward (7)

of *Dancer and Dresser* and *Dressing Room Study*. The other individual portraits and figure studies show varying degrees of 'finish', sometimes effectively juxtaposing heavily worked, detailed areas with more simply realized, lighter shapes. Tom also experiments with untypical pastel textures, brushing water into the powdery pastel colour to dissolve and spread it on a grainy paper, or glazing it onto a smooth ground to form a gentle 'wash' of colour.

This demonstrates both his confidence in handling the medium and a keen sense of the right moment to push a work forward or decide to stop. Two problems that commonly afflict the inexperienced pastellist are, firstly, a reluctance to lose passages that are working well, yet no clear idea of how to pull the rest together; and secondly, a tendency to overwork the surface so that the beautiful colours of the pastels degenerate into a sea of mud. Tom's work shows that the solution to either of these problems is by no means the same in every case. His experience enables him to deal with the 'events' on the surface as they happen, and to judge them in relation to the particular mood and intention of the individual drawing.

DEVELOPING THE IMAGE

Tom feels it is important to understand that, despite the immediacy of pastel, the beautiful and telling effects are not going to come right away of their own accord. It is a matter of practice, exploring the medium and the subject, learning the control, and this takes time. It also means taking a few risks with the things that do go well, and getting a good sense of how one's perception of the subject is interpreted

▲ Dancer and Dresser
1015 × 760 mm (40 × 30 in)

▶ Dressing Room Study
1015 × 760 mm (40 × 30 in)
In both these studies Tom makes a play of the broad shapes that construct the composition, building up the colour impression with a dense massing of hatched and shaded hues and tones. The

balance of tonal values employs the high contrast of black and white, which is echoed by the definite colour contrast of blue and red in the middle-tone range. Sudden, intense bursts of light create the interior glow and emphasize particular details of the figures' forms and textures against the shadowy volumes and deep, dense colours

Ballet Dancer Study

355×255 mm (14×10 in)
*This is a classic piece of pastel
drawing, using the colour of
the paper as the mid-tone
while the pastel colours make
the extremes of light and dark.
There is a beautiful simplicity
to the general pattern of
shapes, with broad strokes in
the dark areas directing
attention to the more complex
colour modelling of the
dancer's body. Blues and
greens mixed into the warm
flesh tints form gently recessed
shadows, which are
counterpointed by the slashes
of pure white and cold blue
emphasizing the contours*

through the medium. He has noted that students can be too tentative about developing the composition and building up colour: 'They get the drawing so far and don't want to lose it, so they tend to work in between the drawing. You have to worry about the structure, getting the structure right, not making it "look like" . . . you have got to mix the colours, not just buy a range of colours and expect to get a match. You learn by making mistakes. Pastel is instant, movable, can be over-mixed, undermixed – you don't have to wait as with paints.'

USING COLOUR

Tom describes colour mixing in pastel as 'mixing while you're working. With oils, you spend so much time on the palette; with chalk, you are working it up, actually drawing.' He remarks that the extensive range of pastel colours in a sense offers too much choice; it is advisable to be selective and apply the palette creatively. 'Pastels are so pure in colour, like a dye that gets into your fingertips; you can break them up and use them as powder or poster colour. Three or four colours give you harmonies and overlays. It's not a matter of putting colours next to one another but of mixing and overlapping.' He makes a comparison with the overprinting technique of lithography, where varying degrees of translucency and opacity cause the colour layers to 'congeal'.

This does involve sometimes sacrificing those attractive, 'working' areas of an image in order to develop the whole: 'All that work, all that drawing, and it's gradually going underneath; but it still gives some lovely colour from underneath, it's quite subtle.' It also means attending

to the interaction of broad shapes and points of detail; Tom describes the effect in a Corot landscape where there is a mass of colour representing the trees and just a few quick, definitive strokes can create the impression of all the variation in the foliage.

At one time, Tom felt himself to be more a tonal painter than a colourist, and there is a strong emphasis on tonal structure in his work that underpins the activity of the colours. But with pastel particularly, he finds it easy to enjoy the colour qualities and is alert to very small, delicate variations as well as the instant impact of the most vibrant hues. As with techniques and surface qualities, he exploits colour differently for different purposes: compare, for example, the heightened, vivid palette of *Kimonos*, set off by the black ground, with the subtler ranges of the individual portraits.

◀ Man in White Pullover
1015×760 mm (40×30 in)
There are few touches of really dark colour in this portrait — the depth of shadows is created mainly with colour gradations and oppositions. It was begun as a demonstration of how to block in a composition and the surface qualities remain fascinatingly loose, even in the face where the colours are layered more densely and a strong impression of detail magically emerges from the meshing of free, multi-directional strokes. One of the beauties of colour mixing in pastels is that it becomes hard to tell which colours are on top, which below; the surface gradually reveals further rich glimpses of the underlayers

▲ Hannah and Me
760×1070 mm (30×42 in)
This delightful double portrait shows the artist painting his daughter. It is an intriguing composition, layering the picture in terms of real space and the mirror-space, and making a rich pattern of the strong hues and dark shadows. It is also a lovely character study of the young model, whose mixed feelings about sitting for the portrait show both on her face and in the tension and implied movement of her pose

Tom Coates is a great ambassador for the medium of pastel, keen to encourage both professional and amateur artists to explore its potential more widely. He promotes it actively through his involvement with the Pastel Society of Great Britain, but offers perhaps his most convincing argument for pastel's exciting versatility in the impressive range of his own work.

MASTERCLASS
with Diana Constance

Every artist's output is shaped by a variety of interests and experiences, but the many different strands of influence that feed into life and work are not always taken up explicitly. Diana Constance has an investigative approach to her drawings and paintings that allows her to connect one kind of interest with another. She has a strong fascination with the technicalities of her media, continually exploring how the physical properties of the materials can be made to work in particular ways, how to build surface effects. On another level, she is working on the possibilities in image-making: both formal concerns about the composition and structure of an image, and ways of conveying narrative or emotional content. Her imagination may be lit by a single, striking photograph, from which a series of drawings emerges; or she may deal with a specific theme, gathering appropriate reference material that clothes the idea.

With regard to the ideas that have contributed to particular works, Diana's references cover a wide range: aspects of her own technique and the qualities of her materials; effects that she has noted and been intrigued by in the work of other artists, or information about their methods; the content of her drawings relating to personal experiences or those of the people who are her subjects; and the large concerns, social and political, that she chooses to confront directly. Her willingness to grapple with painful issues produces some images which, as she readily admits, can be disturbing to look at, but 'art shouldn't be something that stands outside the lives we live'.

▶ Large Head I
710×685 mm (28×27 in)
The pastel rendering began with the bright blue shadow. Diana set herself a major challenge by creating such a powerful impact of shape and colour at this early stage of the work. She allows it full vibrancy by introducing the complementary colour, orange, in a hue not garish, but strong enough to hold its own against the very bright blue.

She continues the bold approach with the heavy black lenses and lush scarlet mouth, varying the pastel textures so that full-strength colour is contrasted with the subtler layering of tones around mouth and chin. The pastel is laid on a tinted acrylic ground, which gives a roughened tooth to the textures. The glamorous quality of the image is immediately striking, but it is a male face, as the strong, muscular modelling reveals

MATERIALS AND TECHNIQUES

Diana's pastels have a powerful, graphic presence that relates directly to the ways she uses her materials. She often begins by drawing in charcoal, or with a charcoal-black soft pastel, to establish a strong tonal structure for the composition before introducing colours. In fact, her starting point for this method is likely to be a small charcoal sketch outlining the darkest and lightest values, from which she moves on to the full-size drawing. She describes being told by a colleague, who had worked with muralists such as Rivera in Mexico, how the vast, complex drawings on the wall were blocked in initially using only Prussian blue for the dark tones, burnt sienna for the mid-tones, and white for the lights, 'so they saw these huge murals as an abstract pattern of just the three major tones. Tones are the most important, the darks and lights, to get that structure right.'

If she uses regular charcoal, which has a lighter texture than that of soft pastel, she may rub the black dust into the surface a little before working over the drawing, otherwise the charcoal can be knocked off by the pastel strokes. Diana uses large blocks of scene-painter's charcoal, rather than the finer artists' sticks. Black pastel makes a heavier, better-quality line than charcoal and is more versatile for blends and textures. Its texture is more stable as the colours are applied.

When the tonal drawing is established, Diana spends time thinking about the colours and how she is going to use them. She selects a colour range from her large tray of pastels and puts the selected sticks into a separate box (she may add a few more as she goes along). One reason for doing this is to see how the colours work together as different tones and colour contrasts; if she feels the balance is wrong, she changes them. The other reason is purely practical: if the selected palette is isolated, Diana doesn't have to spend time looking through the whole tray for the required colours, possibly misjudging which is which as the pastels get dirty and the colours less distinct.

BUILDING UP THE SURFACE

The approach to using colour depends on subject and technique. Over the tonal drawings, Diana describes 'floating the pastel on' or

Victor
680×500 mm $\left(26\frac{3}{4} \times 19\frac{3}{4} \text{ in}\right)$

Victor and Marie Bianchi
685×535 mm (27×21 in)
*These touching, dream-like images evolved out of a book of old photographs (*ABOVE*) left behind by Diana's elderly neighbours, showing the couple at a seaside resort some sixty years earlier.*

*The first drawing of Victor alone (*FAR LEFT*) sets him as a virtual silhouette against the textures of the balustrade and boardwalk. In the second (*LEFT*), Diana began in a similar way, including the decorative detail. However, as the drawing progressed, she decided to knock back that detail and include the second figure, of Victor's wife Marie. To express the fact that Marie had predeceased her husband (though by only a few years), Diana portrays Victor as an older man but shows Marie as the young woman from the seaside photos. The misty ambience evokes a sense of separation and loss*

'veiling' the colours. She also works over acrylic or watercolour grounds, sometimes sweeping the pastel into the paint, other times keeping the media more separate and distinct. Alternatively, she may develop a dense layering of pastel, overlaying colours directly as in *Nude I* and *Victor and Marie Bianchi*. She uses two qualities of soft pastel, keeping the very softest sticks for floating colours into the final surface layers.

61

She uses fixative only when she is layering, but not invariably and only the minimum needed. To apply it or not, and to what extent, is judged according to the effect she is looking for. For example, the strong red underlayer of *Nude I* was not fixed when Diana started to put in the shadow colours; whereas on *Small Head III*, spraying heavily between the layers was part of the technical experiment she made in building up the stone-like texture of the face.

About the way she handles pastel, Diana describes using the stick on its side and moving over the form 'almost as if I'm running my hand, with the pastel, over a face or body. It's a matter of trying to imagine that you're coming over the planes of the face, always moving the pastel with the form, never against it . . . and also trying to make each stroke count. This is very important, because if you lose your concentration, you just start to fill in, you're not actually saying something – so it begins to fall apart very quickly.'

As a teacher of pastel techniques, Diana can identify two particular problems students have with the medium. The first is holding the pastel stick like a pen, so that the strokes are inevitably linear; she advises using the sticks on their sides until the final stages, when the tip can be used to strengthen detail and contour. The second way students disadvantage themselves is by not putting enough colour on the paper: 'Unless you've got a certain amount of pastel, you can't begin to move it; you're not really working one colour into another colour.' But she warns against blending, too much and too soon: 'You can never get the texture back, and you may not need to do it; blending tightens it up. You can just blend parts, and contrast the smooth with the rough textures.'

▲ Nude I
760×535 mm (30×21 in)

▶ Nude II
760×535 mm (30×21 in)
As with Large Head I, the colouring of the first study here (ABOVE) began with a challenge. To establish the impression of strong, hot light, the whole shape of the body was blocked in with brilliant red – the colour now visible only in the hands. Diana then began working the shadow areas with indigo and red oxide, and eventually heightened the lights with vibrant pinks and yellows.

In contrast, the second study (RIGHT), from the same photographic reference, relies strongly on tone and contour. But a similar method of breaking down the forms was used, as the whole surface was originally rubbed with charcoal and the figure shaped as a charcoal line drawing, then the lights were brought up by overlaying the pale pastel tones

▲ 1

▼ 2

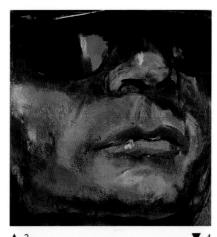

▲ 3

▼ 4

Large Head II

735 × 700 mm (29 × 27½ in)
*Here Diana uses open
techniques which 'scatter' the
colour. She has an abstract
sense of it as she works close
to the surface, then the
portrait pulls together as she
stands back.*

*She begins with a free
charcoal drawing (1) and
floats in some colour, choosing
a high-key palette with no
single dominant hue (2).*

*These colours develop a
different kind of vibrancy from
those of the previous version as
she gradually applies the
pastel layers. The charcoal
still plays a strong part in a
clearly defined tonal structure.
The face is heavily modelled
but the forms are subtly
integrated. Bright lights on the
black lenses create an effect
quite different from the opaque
anonymity they had before,
but one which equally
preserves the menacing aspect
of the concealed gaze (3).*

*At this stage Diana decides
that the image would be more
dramatic if the face were seen
even more closely. She
achieves this by cropping the
drawing to eliminate the
distracting light at the top of
the frame (4)*

THE APPROACH TO THE SUBJECT

When she works from photographs, Diana is often set off by the immediate impact of the picture, as in the *Large Head* and *Small Head* series, but she uses it as a base from which to explore and interpret the image. 'I frequently work on a subject two or three times or more. I find that each time you go into it, you find something completely new and, of course, pastel is very good for this, because it allows you a lot of changes; you can explore ideas very rapidly.' Diana may also make a great many sketches of the subject – bold, informal drawings in felt-tip pen – concurrent with the pastels.

The photographs interest her both for the composition of the shapes and for their moods and associations. She was fascinated by the close-cropping of the picture that inspired *Large Head I* and *II*: 'The fact that the photo was a section of the face makes it slightly aggressive – you're moving into somebody's space and when you're close to somebody else's face it sets up a certain tension. Also, the face has a certain lushness – the lips, the whole thing is very fleshy. I was fascinated that the lips are very lush and sensuous, but the eyeglasses – the fact that the eyes are hidden from you – are very menacing.' The two drawings focus on this strong impression, but Diana uses very different techniques and aspects of pictorial structure to interpret them individually.

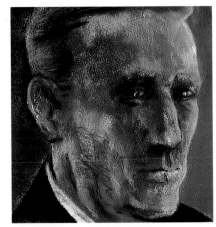

◄ Small Head II

330×330 mm (13×13 in)
A classical approach to tonal
modelling is overlaid with
dramatic tints and highlights,
giving a firmer, more
aggressive character to the
subject. Diana plays off
different qualities of the
medium, using sharp lines
drawn with the pastel tip to
cut across grainy side strokes

▲ Small Head I

330×330 mm (13×13 in)
The disturbing character of
this portrait is deliberate. The
mood is of a man immersed in
tragic circumstances that cast
a hard shadow of guilt and
anxiety – hence the emphatic
line of the darker tones
through the centre of the face
and the schematic arrangement
of discordant colours

◄ Small Head III

330×330 mm (13×13 in)
Diana applies the pastel
densely, with heavy spraying
of fixative on each layer, to
build up a stone-like texture of
closely meshed colours and
tones. A stone portrait
suggests timelessness and
immobility, but the face has
developed a benign expression,
in contrast to the previous two

► Small Head IV

355×330 mm (14×13 in)
The subject of the original
photograph used for this series
of drawings, Mikhail
Bulgakov, was a playwright
and novelist whose work was
suppressed in Stalinist Russia.
From this came the idea of
using red for a striking
monochrome portrait. The red
is laid into charcoal-black
pastel, the whites being mainly
the white of the paper with
some highlighting overlaid.
The reversal of the image
is due to coincidence –
Diana saw the photograph
printed the wrong way round
in a magazine, which
revived her interest in
the theme

For the *Small Head* series, rather than modify the original drawing if a new idea occurred to her, thus losing the evidence of the first idea, she chose to work on several at once so that each could evolve in a different way as new possibilities struck her. None was intended to be a straight-

forward portrait of the subject, Russian writer Mikhail Bulgakov, but Diana used the clarity of the photograph, the strong modelling of the face and, again, the close-cropping of the image, as a means of conveying various associations. Two of the heads took on characteristics of people she knows, although she was not consciously thinking of them. The colour and composition of *Small Head I* is deliberately disturbing, to convey the idea of the shadow of tragedy falling across someone's life; the strong red of *Small Head IV* symbolizes the communist background of Bulgakov's life. But in all the *Heads*, the sense of mood is also expressed directly and almost independently of the idea that is its source, through the organization of shape, colour and texture.

In the landscapes quite different associations come into play. Diana has experience of flying light aircraft: 'My landscapes I really think of as skyscapes; I'm interested in the power, the forces of movement in the air.' She also sketches landscape while travelling, although she never attempts finished works on site. The sketches may be detailed watercolours or monochrome drawings on which she makes comprehensive colour notes. 'I don't copy the sketches; they just sort of feed me ideas. Maybe at a much later date I'll do a work based on the sketches.'

The impression you take from Diana Constance is of a roving curiosity and intelligence to which nothing is inadmissable as material for her art. As much as she is prepared to work through ways of handling difficult subject matter in her paint-

ings and drawings, and think hard about how to express elements of narrative and commentary, she is also deeply involved with the qualities of her materials and the physical properties of colour and texture.

The idea of seeing things through is very important to her. When teaching, she encourages students to finish a drawing, however tempting it may be to abandon it at a disappointing stage. 'If you don't find out what's wrong with it, you're just going to make the same mistake. No matter how much of a mess it gets into, try to work it out. You may be able not only to pull it around, but also see something completely new. If you're making changes, watch what's happening, because you may see something interesting that enables you to continue in a different way.'

Scottish Landscape
520×735 mm ($20\frac{1}{2}×29$ in)
Earlier in her career, Diana's paintings were abstract, and this feeling for abstraction comes through most strongly in her pastel landscapes. She looks for an atmospheric, elemental effect, synthesized with the solid shapes of the land. She achieves this here by wetting the pastel so that the textures vary from the graininess of the clouds to gentle, brushed veils of colour. The drawing is on heavy watercolour paper

▶ Memorial to Dachau

965×675 mm (38×26½ in)
This is one of two drawings
on the same theme – the other
is on exhibition at Dachau.
The idea was to make the
image all-embracing and
protective. Technically, the
powerful monochrome drawing
holds the essence – the boy's
face is kept very simple, with
the features just emerging from
varied pressure in the pastel
strokes. The colour is lightly
'brushed' in, with the paper
surface showing through. The
subject reflects Diana's strong
feeling that her art should
engage with the wider world;
she is interested in using
traditional religious
iconography to address
contemporary issues

▲ Sketches

Diana makes very bold, free
sketch drawings with simple
tools such as charcoal or
felt-tip pen, to explore an idea
and try out ways of
constructing the composition.
She may go over and over the
forms to get shapes, angles
and emphases set in her mind

MASTERCLASS
with Margaret Glass

Margaret Glass regards herself as a painter of light rather than of landscape. 'There must be something in the painting that says why the artist was drawn to paint that subject, and to me, it's light; it's so dominant in my work.' The subject is the 'compositional coathanger' on which she displays the mood of the place as it is affected by the time of day, seasonal light and weather conditions. Often she finds this in an aspect of her immediate locality, which offers low-lying rural landscape and open coastline under enormous skies, so that the quality of light is an acknowledged feature of the region's character. But she is always alert to new subjects and also finds sympathetic moods in places she encounters by chance during holidays abroad.

Sometimes Margaret engages directly with the broad spread of the landscape, particularly in marine views where she is fascinated by the varied effects of light reflecting from the water. But she also seeks out more closely focused pockets of detail, ranging from the enclosed atmosphere of a wooded riverbank where the light is broken and filtered by the trees, to some normally unremarkable corner of a nearby garden or backyard where she finds unusual 'still lifes' formed by the domestic debris. Recently, she has begun to work more frequently on interior views and 'found' still lifes containing furnishings, ornaments and flower arrangements. Here again she composes the picture in a way that centres on the mood of the setting and colouring of the light.

▶ Venetian Doorway
330×240 mm (13×9½ in)
The velvety rich, dark tone of the inset shadow hooked around the doorway pushes up the key of all the pale colours. Margaret employs the oppositions of warm and cool colours to model suggestions of form even where the strong light washes out the intensity of the hues. Notice the brilliance of the pale yellow-greens, offset by the warmth of pink and ochre touches that give an edge to structural details. This direct frontal view of the façade makes a dramatic composition, with nothing distracting from the impact of the characterful doorway. The colours reflected in the murky waters of the canal are hardened and brought down in tone

THE PROPERTIES OF THE MATERIALS

Early in her career, Margaret tried out all the different artists' media, including acrylics, then quite recently introduced, and egg tempera, one of the oldest formulae for paint. She found soft pastel the medium best suited to her temperament and style. She frankly admits that she found it easier to handle than paint, and wanted to bypass the delaying factors of mixing colours and waiting for surfaces to dry. Using pastel, she felt able to work freely and to experiment with technique: 'There were no barriers to how you could use it.

If you know nothing, you're not aware of the limitations.'

From the beginning, Margaret was interested in pastel as a painting medium and wanted to use it as such. She points out that, since Degas, pastel has often been treated more as a drawing tool, with an emphasis on linearity and texture; whereas previously, in the work of artists such as Chardin and Quentin De La Tour, pastel was applied in ways that matched the subtler blending and massing of oil paint. She also acknowledges the 'sculptural' qualities of pastel, the ability to manipulate the substance directly on the surface.

▶ Barge Race off Harwich
480×560 mm (19×22 in)
The excitement of the boats racing through the water put every aspect of this scene into continual motion. This is one of several compositions Margaret worked up from photographic reference, the particular circumstances obviously making it impossible to work on the spot. She has used a view as if from a leading boat looking back on its follower, with the wake of the first boat disturbing the water in the foreground of the painting. She enjoys re-creating the effects of wavelets and ripples on water (see also page 26), using a methodical technique of working light over dark to build up the mixed hues and to finish with the frothy detail and highlighting of the wave crests

◀ Pinmill Foreshore
280×380 mm (11×15 in)
The cold, smoky atmosphere surrounding the boats moored beside a bank of stark trees is organized with a glorious range of muted, pale tints. Darker colours are used to establish definition of forms, but these are allowed to sink into the lights so the tonal range across the surface coheres into an atmospheric haze. The horizontality of the composition also contributes to the image's calm mood; but the eye is led into the landscape by the highlights in the middle ground, and follows towards the literal invitation of the stepped pathway leading into the trees

TEXTURE AND COLOUR

An influential feature of this tactile sense of her medium is Margaret's usual choice of glasspaper as the ground for her work. Its gritty, abrasive surface grips the colour firmly and sometimes causes a true impasto effect – with light from the side, you can see the raised edges of certain strokes where the loose-textured material is thickly deposited on the paper. She mounts the glasspaper on board, so there is an underlying resistance that gives emphasis to the weight and pressure of her strokes.

The abrasive texture of the paper means that the soft pastel can be rapidly used up, and Margaret stresses that it is important not to be miserly in applying the colours. The dense, painterly qualities of her surface effects lead some viewers to suppose that she works in oil pastel, in which the moist binding medium gives a certain lushness to the stroke; but she does not, because she prefers the handling properties of soft pastel and feels that the relatively limited colour ranges of oil pastels are too restricting.

COMPOSING THE PAINTING

Margaret works directly from the subject, composing the image on the spot so that her immediate impression is transferred into the finished painting. She does take photographs for reference, as she works all year round and it is not always practical to be outdoors, but prefers to establish the composition thoroughly while she is at the location. Her aim is to capture the main elements of shape and form and to obtain the 'colour scheme' which is the key to the mood. She may go back to the site under different conditions, to study detail, but she will already have her original idea clearly stated.

Gone for Lunch

240×330 mm (9¼×13 in)

The very ordinariness of this outdoor still life is its attractive quality. There is an interesting harmony in the generally subdued colours, occasionally lit by vivid accents such as the white tyre pump and red reflectors on the bicycle. The man-made machine has a precise construction that is effectively rendered with quite loose, free pastel strokes. Though the bicycle is similar in tone and colour to the rough, repetitive textures of the fencing behind, Margaret brings it out of the background with some very subtle shifts of hue

She works the tonal balance of the painting from dark to light, unless the subject has a misty atmosphere, in which case she reverses the process and goes from light to dark. Her materials partly impose the need for a confident start: on glasspaper, for instance, the dark colours cannot be completely covered. A misplaced stroke can be brushed off but not wholly erased, and its shadow will emerge through overlaid colours.

Margaret understands that it is difficult to find the confidence to make a bold beginning when you are inexperienced in handling pastel. While she was still learning about the medium, she remembers that she tended to start by laying in the middle tones first, to avoid irretrievable decisions, then tried to work the

darks and lights over them. But 'it's got to be strong, bold, right from the start. With placing middle tones first, you don't get the bite on the paper. When you make the first stroke, that's when the colours are most vibrant. When you put one colour on top of another, it sort of sinks into the paper. The first colour you put on is the strongest it will be.'

Although her paintings are usually richly built up, Margaret sometimes leaves glimpses of the bare paper that emphasize the 'bite' – the directions and edge qualities of the strokes – because 'there's a spontaneity there that you just can't get any other way'. This can be seen in the foreground of *Sunlight and Shadow, Venice*. The key thing for someone just starting, she says, is to 'simplify

and look for the basic structure of the painting'. Only through experience do you learn what to put down that really tells in the later stages of the painting: 'People tend to get a lot of extraneous matter that they don't need. It's amazing what you don't need, and what you do.' A careful analysis of the tonal structure, and the right colour key, give Margaret her basic ingredients. On the subject of painting moving water, for example, which can be especially difficult because of its constant changes, she remarks that many people go for the lights first, because an immediate impact comes from the waves breaking at the crests; but her own excellent effects are achieved by sticking to the methodical build-up from dark to light.

Sunlight and Shadow, Venice

280×380 mm (11×15 in)
Soft pastel colours are ideal for capturing those sudden light effects when a shaft of brilliance falls into a shadowy area. It is worth emphasizing the contrasts, not only in the tonal values but also, as happens here, in the intensity of adjacent hues. Much of the picture is painted with colours of a relatively high key, but the interaction of bright yellows and warm ochres against pale, neutral greys and cold blues constructs the light and shade

◀ By the Jetty at Dawn,
Woodbridge
380×280 mm (15×11 in)
*This painting incorporates
two of Margaret's special
preoccupations: marine
subjects, both for the boats
and for the reflected light on
water; and the particular
qualities of light that set the
mood of a scene.*

*She has worked the pastel
layers densely in the upper
part of the picture, pushing the
colours right into the tooth of
the glasspaper ground to form
the ghostly effect of the boat
emerging from the dawn mist.
She achieved this by laying a
base layer of soft pink and
blue, then applying dark
colours over light. In the
foreground, the stronger
contrasts were formed with
direct strokes, light over dark*

▶ Near Coulon
280×380 mm (11×15 in)
*This was a subject discovered
by chance while travelling, so
Margaret had limited time
which forced her to work
quickly and boldly. She
determined to try to avoid
using greens to interpret the
wooded landscape; the range
of greens in soft pastel can be
difficult to handle, often
evading the subtlety and
brightness of nature's own
range. Margaret has relied
mainly on an optical mix of
yellows, blues and black, set
off against the warm sandy
brown of the paper. Her rapid
approach gives the pastel
marks a raw vitality as she
simplifies the detail, working
with quick, incisive strokes
and strong tonal contrasts*

USING COLOUR

The wide range of colours provided
by the best brands of soft pastels
gives Margaret a lavish palette for
painting light effects. She appreci-
ates the vibrancy of the strong hues
and the subtlety of colour variations.
There is a remarkable clarity in, for
example, the difference between a
warm grey and a cold grey, as well
as in more immediately striking contrasts of hue and tone. It fascinates
her that we all have a potentially
unique perception of light and colour. Not only that, but within any
individual artist's frame of reference,
there is the continual activity of colour relationships to be managed and
somehow made to work for a particular painting. 'The juxtaposition
of colours is exciting. It's something
you don't talk about, it just happens
fairly naturally, but the brain is
computing all the while.'

Sometimes Margaret creates a specific challenge for herself, as in the
wooded landscape of *Near Coulon*,
which she wanted to interpret without using greens. At other times she

◀ Eighty Degrees in
the Shade
*240×330 mm $\left(9\frac{1}{2}×13\ in\right)$
The arrangement of elements
within this private garden
corner has a delightfully
incidental character. The
angles of the chair and fence
create a wave-like rhythm,
which is carried off into the
background by the trailing
hosepipe. As the title suggests,
the heat was intense, and this
comes through strongly in the
cast of yellow light*

560×480 mm (22×19 in)
It was not the beauty of the flowers, but of the light effects, that drew Margaret to paint this subject. In the dark shadow of the stairwell, a window opposite threw an angular block of light, against which the well-defined cast shadow of the petunias appears as emphatic shapes with curious edge qualities. The abstract impression of this shadow-play background is pointed up by the naturalistic rendering of the still life

▶ Morning Light, the Hard, Pinmill
480×660 mm (19×26 in)
The colour key of this painting is deliberately pushed to extremes to convey the heat. However, even while intensifying the hot red, orange and yellow range of her palette, Margaret balances these colours subtly with restricted areas containing cooler hues — the olive green trees and slashes of cold blue on the water — and offsets their brightness against enriched, very dark tones

notices a startling effect of light and colour, such as the bright-edged shadow of the flowers against a reflected window of brilliant sunlight in *White Petunias*, that is the trigger for choosing the subject.

Integrated with the strong tonal structure already described, the play of warm and cool colours is a vital element of Margaret's paintings. In this, she is keenly aware that the reference points are never fixed: a rich red, say, that on its own seems naturally warm can turn out to have a cold cast when put down next to another red that reads as brighter and hotter; the 'temperature' of a yellow may depend on whether it stands next to orange or green. She uses these properties to model form and structure in the composition, as well as for their decorative and descriptive functions – and, of course, to create the light.

The stimulus of colours is what gives her a sense of freshness with

each new work, and she is determined never to lapse into easy formulae for using colour. 'In the next
painting, you break the rules you
made in the previous one. Colour-
wise, you can get into a rut. I put
away whatever I've used for the previous painting and start choosing
again from the whole range for the
next subject. It's worth it, because
you forget what you used last time;
you can get just a subtle change and
all the permutations are different.'

MASTERCLASS
with Debra Manifold

Debra Manifold works with pastel for its spontaneity and expressiveness. The essential elements of her paintings are the mood of the image, conveyed primarily through shape and colour, and the variety of the marks that gradually build the atmosphere and detail. She uses the shape and substance of her pastel sticks inventively, making the most of the different qualities of soft, hard and oil pastels. Her techniques exploit the individual materials to the full; she often mixes their textures to excellent effect and also combines paint and pastel freely: 'When I see a subject I instinctively know what mixture of media to use, or whether I'm just going to use pastel.' The energy and variety in the surface effects are underpinned by a strong sense of design, giving the images great dramatic impact.

In the landscape or in the city, Debra is immediately attracted by a view containing large abstract shapes that form an underlying pattern beneath the complexity of the scene. 'It is the mood that I want to get down as much as possible in the first instant', and she sees the mood expressed in the broad pattern of shapes, tones and colours. The paintings are not abstract with the kind of abstraction that can go very far from the original motive, so that the subject disappears from view. In fact, Debra's paintings are wonderfully descriptive, but not in a realist, literal manner.

▶ Blue Monday
525×375 mm $\left(20\frac{3}{4} \times 14\frac{3}{4} \text{ in}\right)$
Debra finds various levels of fascination in this narrow city street: the slightly claustrophobic atmosphere; the material contrasts of new and old buildings; and the layered arrangement of shapes culminating in the wedge of strong light where the sky cuts into the enclosed architecture.

The density of oil pastel is appropriate to the imposing character of the subject and its heavy tones. On the left Debra used turpentine to elide the pastel marks, obtaining the 'shiny, smoothed-out look' of the newly constructed buildings. The structures are reinforced with some emphatic linear marks. She also ran the pastel sticks over areas worked in oil and turpentine that had dried out, which gives the rougher texture and stronger colour contrasts of the old buildings. The vertical gap between the buildings is the focal point, and here the luscious textures are pasted on thickly, activating the surface of the dynamic shape

Entrance to the Forest
305 × 430 mm (12 × 17 in)
Another example of soft pastel over oil paint, this image also gains weight and depth from the materials, enhancing the 'tunnelling' forms of the trees. This deliberate heaviness is strikingly counterpointed both by the bold handling of pale tints and acid hues, and by the way the sweeping curves within the foreground open out the view

A PATTERN OF SHAPES

Debra's interest in the abstract qualities is a matter of getting to the fundamental elements: the weight and mass of permanent structures; the skeletal frameworks of natural and man-made environments; powerful atmospheres resonant with lights and shadows and washed in beautiful colours. She describes what she is looking for as 'that larger-than-life sense of things'.

She may see an exciting subject and not do anything about it for a while, just letting herself live with the picture in her mind – 'the parts

that stick' will become the essence of the composition. When she is ready to start work, she may go back to the location and gather more reference, but the main aim of the painting is to recapture the immediacy of that first impression.

Sometimes she works directly with only the most basic visual ingredients – perhaps limiting her palette severely and dealing almost exclusively with strong but simple shapes. At other times she achieves the right effect by working through the possibilities for complicating the image, then revising the balance of the picture and knocking out what seems to

Seclusion

510×380 mm (20×15 in)
By underpainting with thin layers of oil paint, Debra lays in a substantial textural base that gives body to the picture. She used the paint to establish the rhythm of the abstract shapes and allowed it to dry before starting to draw with soft pastel. The free movement and grainy layering of the pastel marks build solidly on the painted foundation, but the underlayers show through in places. This effect enhances the depth of the semi-enclosed landscape view and creates interesting variations of colour and texture

be extraneous detail. 'Before I've started painting it, there is that abstract quality, so that if you took away all the things that progress throughout the painting, there would be that initial pattern. . . . A sort of ideal would be to get back into the abstract pattern again, so that when you've put in all the detail, you go back to that initial state; but it's perhaps more sophisticated than it was at first, because you have done the detailed work.'

Debra regards pastel as the perfect medium for this working method because it allows her to progress so quickly: 'You can do it at the same time as the thought processes, while you're painting.' She doesn't want to be slowed by having to mix colours or waiting for surfaces to dry; she enjoys the immediacy and direct-ness of pastel colour, the fact that the medium itself encourages the spontaneous development of the painting.

MAKING MARKS

The forcefulness of the shapes is particularly apparent in *Le Soir Animé* and *Dockhead*, both subjects that display a monumental presence, but it is interesting how different the approaches to each painting are. In *Le Soir Animé* the trees and the land are portrayed as heavily massed forms; their shapes have density and inner movement, drawn from the rich colours and a gentle fusion of the pastel marks that occurs despite the active, emphatic qualities of individual strokes. In *Dockhead* the whole texture is harsher, in keeping with the mood of the industrial location. The powerful black and white contrast puts all attention on the characteristics of the marks, and the linear structure coheres as a matted network of dashing strokes. These treatments create distinctive atmospheres: the wooded landscape is stark but in its way inviting; the landscape of the docks is hard, jarring, even dangerous.

Although all of the images are alive with the gestural and tactile qualities of Debra's techniques, the mark-making is particularly important when she works primarily with tonal values; then she relies on the pastels' range of contact with the paper, rather than the colour, to convey the mood. 'Dockhead was all about the emphasis of the marks. There was colour; some people might choose to paint that scene in subtle variations of grey – that would be wonderful, but I'd choose to express that by the variation of marks, punctuating the heavy parts to balance it up, being subtle or definite in certain areas.'

▲ Le Soir Animé

560×685 mm (22×27 in)
This 'monumental' clump of trees is a fine example of the underlying abstract forms that attract Debra's eye to a composition. The essence of that first dramatic impression is preserved by emphasizing the large, simple shapes that the trees create against the skyline. She blocked in the overall shape in monochrome, then worked up the vibrant reds and yellows very lightly in layers over the dark mass, building up the textures and colours with bold, spontaneous strokes in soft and hard pastels. By adding touches of blue, white and grey, she lets just enough light into the trees to explain the branching within the main shapes

▶ Dockhead

735×535 mm (29×21 in)
The aggressive shape of the crane starkly etched against the skyline made an irresistible subject. Debra chose to work very rapidly and spontaneously in black and white, with only occasional punctuations of colour. The monochromatic approach enabled her to focus on the exciting variation of the marks, with nothing distracting from the strong abstract structure of the composition. She worked first in oil pastel, varying the pressure to stress the most important heavy, balancing areas. The surface was then reworked with soft pastel and compressed charcoal, making use of the ways oil resists the looser texture of the dry pastel, which skips over the surface, forming broken colour effects with random, torn textures

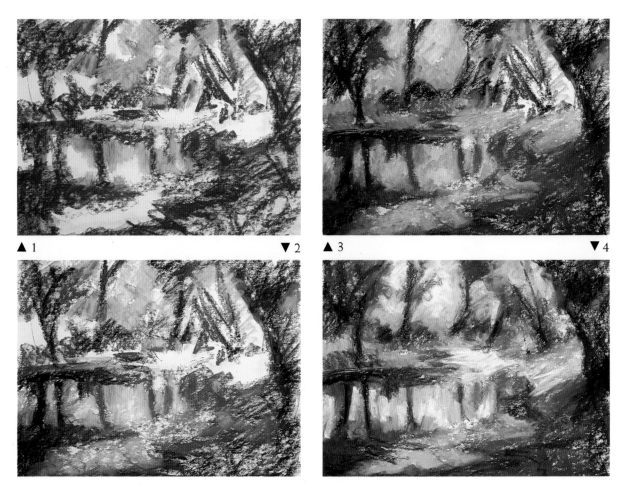

▲ 1 ▼ 2 ▲ 3 ▼ 4

Forest Glade

405×535 mm (16×21 in)
*Debra blocks in the overall
composition with grainy
strokes, using the side and tip
of the soft pastels (1).*

*The colours are selected to
provide a basic pattern of
tonal values. She is working
on a neutral, light-coloured
mount board and its surface
acts as the lightest tone at this
stage. She continues to build
up the shape of the image
loosely, developing the
contrasts with the insertion of
black and pale blue (2).*

*As the colour range
increases, enhancing the lights
and shadows, so the texture of
the surface becomes more
complex and the marks begin
to mesh and blend (3).*

*The colours Debra has
used up to now form a sort of
underpainting and she begins
to orchestrate the changes,
strengthening the structure of
the composition and
introducing white to heighten
the contrasts (4).*

*She works back and forth
across the painting, allowing
the directions of the pastel
strokes to build form and
atmosphere, as well as
intensify the colours (5).
Some strokes are deliberately
linear and sharp, to create
points of focus.*

*In the final stage, she
inserts a dramatic shift of key,
using warm yellows,
red-browns and muted pinks
to cast the light more strongly,
contrasting them with vivid
touches of blue and playing
the bright colours across the
darkness of the black
underpainting (6)*

▲ 5

▲ 6

Debra keeps a sheet of paper beneath the pastel painting, on which she tests the colours as she selects them, to check the qualities of hue and tone and to judge them against the colour interactions already established in the composition

USING THE MATERIALS

One way in which Debra achieves the variety of a surface is by selecting different kinds of pastels – and also charcoal and paint media – that respond to characteristic features of the subject. She uses swathes of soft pastel, applied with the side of the stick, to glaze a landscape with the glow of evening light; she will choose a hard pastel to point up the boniness of a tree root poking through the ground; she employs the sticky, heavy texture of oil pastel to

supply the gravity of an imposing subject. She combines materials that fuse and blend, and materials that resist each other. But she can also extract many different kinds of marks from each medium, so the possibilities are infinite. 'It is all to do with the mood and expressing something; to do with the physical thing of creating', both in the materials and 'the way you move on the paper'.

Debra also experiments with different kinds of grounds for her paintings, not only with the given colours and finishes of paper or board but also by applying underpaintings that promote a particular feel to the image from the start. Quite unusually, she will lay soft pastel over a ground of oil paint; these media are not natural partners, but she likes to get the density of oil paint as a basis for certain subjects. She also mixes soft and oil pastels, and plays with the random textures that occur as the dry medium adheres irregularly to the oily base.

WORKING WITH COLOUR

Another reason for mixing media is the variations of colour that become available. Oil pastels are characteristically different from soft pastels because the oil base makes the

85

Autumn Flame

560×685 mm (22×27 in)
A haunting mood is evoked
by the exposed and
'petrified-looking' trees,
stripped bare of their summer
foliage. Struck by the contrast
between their cold, naked
forms and the warm autumn
colours around them, Debra
treated the trees primarily as
negative shapes. She worked
loosely in broad, thin
watercolour washes of browns,
reds and yellows, blocking in
the surrounding colours. The
background and foreground
were built up in pastel around
the trees and she then worked
with short, spiky, upward
strokes on both trees and
background, to pull the two
elements together

colours glossy and gives a slight translucency; this contrasts with the colour opacity and velvety, matt or grainy textures of soft pastel. Debra works hard pastels over soft to sharpen the colour intensity, as well as the texture of the marks. She finds that there are some particularly bright, vibrant hues in hard pastels that lift the colour impression, and because the marks are harder, this can be exploited even when the hue is similar to that of the soft pastel over which it is applied. Generally, she uses the hard pastels right at the end of the painting, to enhance the emphasis.

Debra likes to use colour boldly: 'Because of the abstract qualities, if there is dark it has got to be contrasted by strong light. I tend not to be attracted to subtleties. . . . Colour is something to convey mood; it's an emotional thing. So the colours do tend to be on the bright side; I'm aware that's what I'm putting down.'

The light is a very important quality of the paintings, and this can lead her to work with quite extreme contrasts of tone and strong colour 'temperatures'. Where there is warm light, she may include vivid, hot pinks and oranges, gold and scarlet, sometimes set against heavy, deep greens for contrast. Colder atmospheres come through in acid greens and yellows, touches of icy blue, and subtle, cool greys. These are underpinned with a range of earth colours, varying from warm ochres and siennas to dark, restrained umber and sepia. Both the muted and the singing colours are often integrated with strong blacks.

Even when the colour range is tightly restricted, there is tension and activity derived from powerful oppositions of tone and hue. The palette is naturally suggested by the character of the subject – the city paintings are, for example, generally more austere than the wooded landscapes. But in *Blue Monday* the townscape greys are lit with flashes of bright colour that give an appropriate sense of changeability and a 'populated' feel to the narrow street.

A SENSE OF FRESHNESS

The organization of colour relates to the abstract impression, the pattern of shapes that Debra works with from the beginning. She looks to convey both these elements simply and strongly: 'Because you have all these readily available colours that you don't have to mix, it's very easy to pick up lots of colours and start putting them on the paper, so it very quickly becomes muddy and clogged up. It is important to be selective in your colours to start with, and to keep it as simple as possible, but with a variation of marks.'

After the Storm

500×380 mm $\left(19\frac{3}{4} \times 15\ in\right)$
The resist technique of soft pastel over oil perfectly evokes a shimmering rain-washed atmosphere, but a hint of sunlight breaking through is created by the particular combination of warm earth colours and luminous, cold greys. The colours also represent the gritty character of the riverside inner-city landscape, with its ageing structures overlooked by tall modern buildings

She stresses how essential it is to keep the spontaneity and freshness, avoiding the temptation to create a formula out of approaches that have previously proved successful. There are instinctive responses in each artist that need to be allowed to come through in the work – in the attraction to a particular subject, in the choice of materials and colours, and the techniques of developing the composition. This is why Debra is constantly exploring the effects of different grounds, ways of handling the pastels, and mixed-media techniques. 'The idea of consciously following a formula, it will work for a certain amount of time, then it becomes just that. Once you get stuck into a formula you can't progress. You have to get basic knowledge, and then always progress from that.'

MASTERCLASS
with Geoff Marsters

Painting is a process of continual decision-making – what to paint, which materials to use, how to apply the characteristics of the medium to the information in the subject. Occasionally, such decisions have an unexpectedly large significance; one specific choice can take an artist into a whole new territory. This happened to Geoff Marsters, who started working with pastels after a long period of consciously avoiding the medium. That choice triggered a totally absorbing exploration of pastel techniques and effects that has lasted several years.

Geoff had previously rejected pastel because he thought of it, from the examples he had seen, as typically a medium for colour drawing, and this approach did not interest him. What started him off was examining the pastel works of Degas in the course of teaching art history to his students: 'I thought, I've got to do something with this – it was as simple as that. But I determined right from the beginning that I was going to try and paint with it.' He began with oil pastel, but found it too restricting. Moving to soft pastel, he experimented freely with techniques; never having had any instruction on how to use the medium, he felt no inhibitions about 'just playing'. He enjoys the way pastel allows the artist direct physical contact with the colours and textures – 'there's not even a brush between you and it'. His paintings are a continuous experiment in handling the medium. Although he has evolved techniques that enable him to achieve particular effects he is looking for, it is apparent that his work keeps progressing.

▶ Boathouse Interior
760×560 mm (30×22 in)
Coming across this subject by chance, Geoff was initially fascinated by the chaotic detail, but as he began to make sketches he found that a 'working order' emerged.

The dark interior was lit by skylights above and cluttered windows to one side, creating random patterns of light and shadow. Geoff deals with this by translating the explosive linear structure in terms of emphatic contrasts of hue and tone, using black as a colour value rather than merely to form a graphic framework. A strong sense of drawing is essential to find the pictorial order; that structural element keeps returning through the colour work. Importantly, however, the technique is directed towards integrating the colour with the drawing, not superimposing one on the other

Sketchbook drawings
Geoff's pencil sketches are surprisingly economical, sometimes with a fragile, exploratory quality. He tries to begin a sketch with the part of the view that made the first impact, which acts as a trigger for the rest. It is a process of distilling the right kind of information — he seeks out the essence of the subject and the factors that, back in the studio, will both evoke clear memories of the scene and provide workable formal elements

FINDING THE SUBJECT

The raw material of Geoff's work comes from his habitual practice of sketching likely subjects on location. He spends days and days drawing in the countryside or on the coast, at home and abroad, and fills dozens of sketchbooks. In this way he can acquire a large series of visual notes on a single theme, but they do not all equally suggest a follow-up in pastel. He looks for the sketches that definitely show his response to the immediate impact of the subject: 'I find the only ones I can use are the ones that have that quality, and have been worked confidently and boldly.

Raybel at Pinmill

495×665 mm (19½×26¼ in)

Although looking for a descriptive rendering of the subject, Geoff was not thinking of it in terms of the fact that it is a boat of a certain type. He was drawn into the formal elements very strongly – the directions and placing of verticals and horizontals; where there is mass and volume; where there is line.

By positioning the weight of the major shapes at the centre of the composition, he presents himself with a dominant focal area that requires him to organize the balance of the image very carefully. This is created by taking the linear structures upwards and outwards, and by offsetting subtle colours with stronger hues and tones. The vertical pastel strokes in the sky are an unusual solution to the problem of how to activate broad colour areas, but Geoff felt the hand movement came entirely naturally

Those in which I seem to draw back into being over-conscious, over-careful, I never want to work from them. But having said that, some sketches do really take a lot of analysis and thought.'

It is important to Geoff that he has a strong feeling about the subject, which may be defined in different ways. The paintings are clearly a means of expressing a true sense of the location and its given mood when the artist first saw it. These things firstly come through in the shape of the landscape as he describes it: the flat spread of fenland or open coast and the broad skies; the vertical and horizontal layerings of rising land; the densely massed forms of trees in full leaf and blossom. Within these shapes he builds up a suffusion of colours and lights that convey local atmosphere.

Sometimes, however, he is conscious of responding quite objectively to formal visual qualities, such as a particular configuration of shapes in landscape or the hardened patterns of man-made structures, as in *Raybel at Pinmill* and *Boathouse Interior*. These also reflect a strong subjective element – the artist's love of boats – but the latter, especially, is extremely demanding in formal terms. It has a mass of details that have to be unravelled in order to create the framework of the painting; at the same time, Geoff deals with the fragmenting of colours and tones that occur because of the different light sources penetrating the dark interior. And when these formal elements are satisfactorily organized, the picture becomes, of course, most atmospheric.

Geoff suggests that an apparently instinctive response may carry in it that appreciation of formal elements: 'I say to students, "Don't bother about the subject. Just go out and sit, and something will take your attention." Now, probably, that's the thing to go for . . . the "something" is going to depend on you, your feeling, and your likes and so on – but probably within that, there's a formal thing going on; it may be just a contrast of light, shadow, shape, whatever.' But however he analyses the particular attraction of a subject, Geoff feels that fundamentally what he is looking for is the core, the essence of it.

BUILDING A SURFACE

Geoff has tried many different kinds of papers to test their influence on the painted surface. The especially rich, dense qualities of colour and texture characteristic of his work are now obtained by applying the soft pastels to pumice paper, an abrasive, heavily toothed surface that

enables him to build layer upon layer. He has an unusual but highly effective method of producing the atmospheric blends and veils of colour. He applies the pastel heavily and rubs it right into the abrasive surface using kitchen paper. One layer is fixed and another laid on top and rubbed down; the process is repeated, often several times, until he sees the right effect. He then works with direct strokes onto the ground of pastel, to retain a feeling of freshness in the final image and bring back the luminosity. Because the tooth of the pumice paper is not completely filled by the rubbing down, the overlaid strokes still have variable thicknesses and edge qualities that act descriptively.

Rubbing and blending the powdery medium risks muddying the hues. The application of fixative, which is necessary when so much pastel is going onto the surface, also dulls the colours significantly. So Geoff has had to find out by trial and error how to make this technique work. He uses less fixative now than previously and does not always fix

▶ Pont C'hoat, Brittany
405×535 mm (16×21 in)
This scene is beautifully typical of the Breton landscape in spring, with the generous spread of pink and white blossom trees brightening the mood. The composition takes up an echo of the pale trees in the tiny white houses close to the horizon. The depth of the picture comes from a more or less banded arrangement of the colours identifying receding elements of the space. The foreground forms are simplified and darkly contoured, to contain the dancing strokes within the shapes

◀ Shaded Pool
340×420 mm (13½×16½ in)
The colour harmony is a natural indicator of the serene character of the location. The mood is further contained within the soft gestures of the pastel strokes. There are no hard edges or distinctive contrasts – the tones are very subtly keyed to bring up definition of the forms. The impression of 'backlighting' is effectively employed to lead the eye right through the image

the final surface, but he still finds it necessary to develop the intensity and contrast of colours and tones more powerfully because they will be knocked down when the fixative goes on. He candidly admits to having lost whole paintings through overworking the surface, but 'it's only through feeling one's way, exploring, and making mistakes, that one actually moves'. Both the successes and the failures provide 'a stage in finding things out'.

The method is not invariable; in some paintings Geoff works directly onto the paper without rubbing down. Even when he is using that heavy blending technique, he devises different ways of rubbing the colour to vary the textures and colour interactions. But the sheer quantity of pastel put down is normally an important part of building the mood and atmosphere of the painting, and it does require the specific properties of the pumice paper ground. Pastel and watercolour papers, even those that have a pronounced tooth, simply do not hold the required amount of colour.

COLOUR AND COMPOSITION

On account of certain attitudes absorbed during his training and early career, Geoff never felt great confidence in using colour boldly. As he started to work in soft pastels, the fact that the medium provides such a broad palette of particularly vibrant, unmixed colours was part of the challenge. As with technique, this is something he has gradually learned to exploit to the full: for example, in the dazzling high-key colours of *Fen Cottage* and the dramatically contrasted tones and hues of *Boathouse Interior*. He describes it as a great adventure to explore 'this fascination of colour relationships that relate to the landscape, yet are independent of it'.

The colour decisions are located in the actualities of the subject and also its mood, but move into independence as the surface qualities of the painting develop. Geoff enjoys the subtleties of landscape as well as the obviously impactful elements. In *Fen Cottage* the brilliant colours and broad shapes are immediately strik-

ing, but Geoff also speaks of focusing his interest on the tonal balance at the horizon, where the distant trees fade into almost the same tone as the sky, 'because the light penetrated behind the middle distance'.

In *Norfolk Coast*, he was taken with the simplicity of the landscape: 'gentle sweeps of movement, that's all it is really, with just enough tonal and colour change to make it actually work in space. The subject itself is so simple that the formal visual content has to be fascinatingly varied with, for example, the sky changing all the way over, and all the way down, with no repetition. The sea is changing across its whole width, and the sunlight, the balance of tones, light to dark, right to left – all these interchanges over large areas, subtly varying.' His ideal is a kind of flexibility that 'lets the subject flow through the colour'.

▶ Fen Cottage
560×760 mm (22×30 in)
The colour hits the surface very directly in this painting. There was no long process of blending; the strokes were freely overlaid to build up form and texture. Geoff laid in the darker tones and a small amount of linear work, then 'smashed in' the colours on top. The pumice paper used has a rippling grain within the fabric, as well as its abrasive surface tooth, which he wanted to use positively. He has exploited it to obtain the shimmering pattern of light across the sky and the rolling texture of the land. The brilliant colours were suggested by a strong yellow cast in the fields after harvest, and by the warmth and light. Yellow thus forms the key colour, which has been played up as the dominant hue and vibrantly mixed with complementary purples and soft pinks

▶ Norfolk Coast

560×760 mm (22×30 in)
*The shapes of the flat, open
coastline are barely suggested
through the gradual blending
of gentle colours. Then
sudden, dramatic strokes, such
as the shaft of pale colour
across the beach, start to
define the space. Such
occasional slight hardening of
the linear and edge qualities
within the veils of pastel
colour creates the sense of
distance in the landscape, as
well as the simplified forms of
the coastal scenery. Geoff likes
to work with compositions in
which there is 'less and less
content', with which he can
do 'more and more to develop
the feel and atmosphere of
the space'*

95

Ivaara

405×535 mm (16×21 in)
This is an example of the kinds of wild landscape especially attractive to Geoff, owing to their bleakness and simplicity. These qualities challenge him to devise formal equivalents for the subtle emphases of the view. He describes the strata of the land in horizontal bands shot through with shifting verticals. These vertical marks pulling upwards through the horizontal stresses create the sense of unity between land and sky that Geoff is seeking

Creating space with colour, rather than through a defined perspective, has been a special preoccupation for Geoff. In this context he refers to Cézanne's paintings, which he loves. The composition of *Ivaara* irresistibly recalls Cézanne's series on *Mont Sainte-Victoire*, although it has its own logic arising from the landscape of northern Finland and is not directly influenced by the French painter.

CREATING SURFACE INTEREST

The exact character of the marks is as crucial to that painting as the orchestration of colours, and this is another strong feature of Geoff's approach to composition. Although he varies the direction, weight and emphasis of the pastel strokes across the surface, he likes to work towards a unified effect. This is not a kind of uniformity that could deaden the picture, but a sense of cohesion in which disparate elements coalesce. With the marks, as with the colours, particular relationships emerge that hold the tensions and balances of the image.

In *Raybel at Pinmill* the touch and movement of the pastel contributes to a fairly literal interpretation of the subject; in the *Untitled* abstract, based on a sketch of a wooded river, the artist explores the exuberance of the colours and marks in their own right.

▲ Untitled
650×495 mm $\left(25\frac{1}{2} \times 19\frac{1}{2} in\right)$

◀ Blue River
650×495 mm $\left(25\frac{1}{2} \times 19\frac{1}{2} in\right)$
*In both these paintings,
extracted from similar
riverscape views, Geoff obtains
the gradual cohesion of the
surface by maintaining
consistency in the character of
the marks. Blue River
(ABOVE) is the more
descriptive in its atmospherics,
both the colour and
shimmering texture evoking the
partial concealment of the
watery location; while in the
untitled painting (LEFT),
Geoff exploits fully the marks'
'independence of the subject'
and goes all out for a joyous,
colourful mood. Despite the
freedom of the abstract
interpretation, the essential
movements came from the
sketch made at the location*

Geoff is intrigued by a kind of paradox the artist has to face: 'I feel that the subject is terribly important, but equally, so is the paint quality and what one does with it. For me, at the moment, painting is three things: it's the subject, it's the medium, and one's own response to these. So one is immediately in the position of working with contradictions – does the subject take pre-eminence, or does the medium? I don't want to lose the subject, I don't want to lose the medium, and I find that fascinating.'

MASTERCLASS
with Ken Paine

The term 'modelling' is commonly used to describe the painter's process of re-creating three-dimensional form and volume on a flat surface. In the case of Ken Paine's portraits, the word returns more truly to its sculptural sense – his subjects are modelled with a real sense of substance. The tactile qualities are intense: he shows you the exact shape of the head; the hard pressure of the bones beneath the skin; the tautness or slackness of facial muscles; the dips, hollows and wrinkles on the surface of a 'lived-in' face or the clear features of a youthful model. Ken is a romantic with a strong sense of theatre; he looks for the drama of a composition. The poses are expressive, and presented expressively to the viewer – Ken's people can come at you with a fierce momentum, or settle back into the paper in total repose.

In using pastel, he says, 'you have the advantage of the sculptor'. The pastellist is literally in touch with the colour and texture of the materials, and with the fabric of the painting. The directness of the medium is inspirational. 'You don't have to mix your colours, squeeze your tubes out, you just pick up a colour. It's a spontaneous feeling; you can put it all down in one go.'

▶ The Jazz Musician
760×585 mm (30×23 in)
It is fascinating to see how Ken's loose, informal technique constructs such a precise evocation of character and mood. Even in a quiet, thoughtful pose, he uses active pastel textures to convey the musician's heavy head and features, and his weary expression. This sympathetic portrayal has a sombre tone, but it is lifted by the strong directional light and vibrant, cold tints in the shadows

FINDING THE SUBJECT

Watching Ken at work, you have the sense that a knowledge of his subject flows straight out of his fingertips. There is a kind of magical communication as a head and face emerges from the rapid movements of the pastel stick; and not just a face, but that particular face, with all its character inherent. But it doesn't do to regard it as some kind of conjuring trick – the truth of the portrait comes both from Ken's skills of observation and technique, and from his remarkable openness to each new model. His long experience does not prompt him to make assumptions. 'Every portrait is an adventure; they are all completely different, and I approach each one with that in mind: this is a challenge, this is an adventure.'

The quickness and confidence of his technique is impressive, but the activity comes in phases. In the times in between, Ken is sometimes quite immobile while he studies the model carefully, looking and thinking. He will, as he says, just stand and stare for long periods: 'The art is looking three times, and drawing once.' He also watches intently the portrait he has made. Like any good artist, he is constantly dealing with that dialogue between the character of the subject and the character of the painting as a thing in itself.

Many people find portraiture difficult because of the mixture of subjective and objective responses. They can't quite lose the sense of the person enough really to see the simple physical attributes; or if they do, it can go too far and the portrait loses its life. Ken's work invariably fuses the personality with the physical structures, and he finds the framework of the portrait by the intensive observation that he insists is the key.

Elderly Gentleman
610 × 455 mm (24 × 18 in)
The densely detailed layering of this portrait is typical of Ken's energetic style, but individual marks occasionally hesitate and fracture, in keeping with the fragile physique of the subject. The technique beautifully captures the strange quality of an aged face in which the shapes and features are at the same time more pronounced and less distinct than they were in the person's youth

The Businessman

610 × 455 mm (24 × 18 in)

Ken works at first in monochrome, going back and forth across the paper, finding the essential shapes and tonal structure of the face (1).

He then deals with the complementary areas, enhancing the pattern of light and shadow (2). His strokes are quick and confident: he uses mainly the side of the pastel stick and angles it briefly to create more emphatic edge qualities. He advises using the 'bulk' of the pastel to develop the form — 'there is plenty of time for pointing up in the final stages'.

After spending a long time on the primary structure, he starts to strengthen the tonal balance, modelling the deep shadows and hard lines of the face in black, and the mid-tones in strong red-orange (3).

Extending his palette, he works rapidly across the face, touching in vivid colour accents and intense points of light (4). The textural qualities are also increasingly complex, with grainy side strokes overlaid by rich impasto (5).

He finishes with free, scribbled strokes that bring out the shape of the head against the background, and some calligraphic flourishes that point up the solidity of the face by contrast (6)

▲ 1

▲ 4

▲ 2　　　　　▼ 3

▲ 5　　　　　▼ 6

STRUCTURING THE PORTRAIT

Ken describes looking for the 'attractive area or areas' of the subject. In any pose, whether the model is looking up or down, or is seen full face or from the side, there is 'always a beautiful area that needs more attention than other parts. There are certain areas that you can virtually leave untouched; it's better if you skim over them and let these carry the parts that are accentuated.'

This impression of a definitive focal point is something that occurs in every subject – landscape or still life, for example, as well as portraits. Finding the right emphasis for each part of the rendering is 'like looking into a tunnel; there's a beginning and an end, the end of the tunnel being the dramatic impact of the portrait'. But with all his experience and confidence, Ken acknowledges that it can be difficult to recognize the key areas, to find a pose that accommodates and accentuates the detail, and enables you to achieve the balance of the portrait. He advises that you find these things only by working at it, if necessary doing it again and again.

The basic shapes and rhythms of the pose are the first essentials. The shapes, not the details, are the most immediate means of recognition, provided they are exact. As is evident from the first stage of Ken's demonstration portrait (see page 101), this has nothing to do with photographic exactness but with the sensation of form – line, mass, rhythm – which he interprets first through tonal values. Using only one or two colours, he blocks in a pattern of light and shadow that builds up into a solid presence. He can spend a long time on this stage, sweeping in grainy colour layers with broad side strokes, changing

the angle and pressure of the pastel stick momentarily to strengthen the tones and create occasional linear emphasis.

Ken explains that it is not worth continuing a portrait if these basic shapes are not right, because everything else builds on them. Once the structure is in place, he progresses the portrait by looking for the shapes within shapes, then further breaking down the detail. All the time, he allows the movement of the pastel to respond directly to what he sees, using rapid, instinctive, rhythmic strokes.

◄ The Thinker

735×535 mm (29×21 in)
The velvety texture of soft
pastel is fully exploited in the
dark, underlying structure of
the face and head, but this
characteristic quality of the
medium is brilliantly
counterpointed by the spiky
sculpting of the hair. Ken uses
the tip and edge of the pastel
stick to achieve crisp linear
strokes and angular highlights
on the face's bony planes.
Because of the intensity of the
modelling, it comes as a
surprise that the colour range
of the portrait is so severely
restricted

► The Opera Lover

965×760 mm (38×30 in)
Ken describes the profile
portrait as 'the most difficult
of all angles, but very fine
and arrogant when it comes
off. One must work very hard
on the silhouette to achieve a
good likeness.' He also chose
this view for the opportunity
to make the most of the
subject's magnificent
moustache. The detail picture
(BELOW RIGHT) shows the
complex pattern of directional
strokes used to build these
elements of the portrait, and
the bright colours applied to
the flesh tones, which vibrate
against the strong tonal
structure of the whole
composition

CHOOSING A PALETTE

The tonal structure of the portrait underpins the detail and surface colour. Ken frequently works in monochrome, or in closely related colours that create a monochromatic impression, as in *The Thinker*. He favours warm browns – sepia and sanguine shades – and hot, strong reds that can dissolve into orange, crimson or deep pink. He has a remarkable way with brilliant yellows, never the easiest colours to handle, sometimes splashing the illumination onto a portrait with bold, abandoned strokes.

Ken says you will gravitate to your own palette eventually, and certain colours will become personal favourites – 'all the artists in the world don't use all the colours in the world'. Although he has a selective palette of his own, he likes to mix colours up on the paper surface, especially in the final stages of a full-colour portrait. His colours are not naturalistic, but they derive from particular cues in his subject. He will intensify the reds where the model is seen in warm light, which creates the heavy strong mood in *Canadian Treefeller*; and inserts scintillating cold, pale blues or limy greens into the shadows, as can be seen in *The Jazz Musician*. He often does the unexpected – for example,

running calligraphic trails of pure primary colours, such as bright ultra-marine, yellow and vermilion, across the subtle, earthy tones of the underpainting. Somehow, it all meshes together and the portrait looks real.

He believes in using colour intuitively: 'It will soon let you know if it doesn't work. Don't dispense with your colour spectrum altogether, but don't be a slave to it.' He compares the experience of working with colour to that of knowing the anatomy of a portrait: 'You're not going to draw the bones, you're going to draw the face.' In the same way, once you have learned something about your colours and you know what they can do, that knowledge

The Old Soldier
685×1015 mm (27×40 in)
The dynamic force of the image lies in the sheer bulk of the giant old man, which has been woven from the all-over mass of active strokes. The board was first painted with gouache, applied with a 50 mm (2 in) housepainter's brush, so that the surface already had a strong textural feel

Canadian Treefeller
810×990 mm (32×39 in)
The highly active acrylic ground establishes beautiful, loose gradations of hot colour over which Ken attacks the portrait as a monochrome drawing. A combination of black and red is one of the strongest, most graphic partnerships in the colour spectrum, which together with the harshly textured pastel strokes builds a tough, dominating image

becomes a springboard for a more adventurous approach. Ken warns against using colours in a certain way because of the influence of a fashionable style, or because someone has told you to do so, but 'do experiment, because if it looks right, it is right. End of story.'

MATERIALS

Ken generally uses soft pastels, and can manipulate them in ways that actively express the variations of form and texture in a portrait – the soft fleshiness of cheeks and jowls or the hard, bony structures of brow and chin. He rarely rubs or blends the colours with his fingers; the grad-

ual overlaying of strokes causes them to merge where required without muddying.

He emphasizes being prepared to make generous use of the materials: 'You may use up one pastel in three or four strokes, but the end product is worthwhile.' He advises using inexpensive papers while learning your craft, then, as you gain confidence, you can move on to special pastel papers or handmade sheets, choosing suitable textures and colours. Ken applies pastel direct to paper or board, and also sometimes over grounds that he has brushed on in gouache, watercolour or oil. For certain portrait moods, he 'wet-brushes' the soft pastel to spread the colour into fluid tinted washes.

Caribbean Woman
810×535 mm (32×21 in)
This was a reluctant model, so
Ken was forced to work very
quickly – hence the vigorous
textures of the strokes. He
focused on trying to catch the
unsmiling, proud expression
during the brief pose, and to
bring out the flavour of the
Caribbean colours with a
limited palette much less bright
than they actually appeared

WORKING WITH THE SITTER

Portraiture has some specific requirements. Every viewer is experienced in looking at faces – we all do it all the time – and a portrait has to be in some senses correct and convincing, even when we don't know the sitter. Obviously, Ken's work does not resolve this need for identification by retailing a minutely detailed likeness. He deals with the mood and energy of the moment, reflected in his exuberant mark-making, while also attending to the particularities. He describes a reciprocal honesty between artist and sitter: 'It's all there in portraiture; it does exist. This is the thing about portraits – everything exists. You get the best you can out of the person – there must be an element of truth.'

It is natural for the viewer to focus on the head and face in a portrait, looking for the character there as one does in life. Many of Ken's paintings concentrate on the head, but he is constantly aware of the whole person and how people present themselves. In his close-up portraits, the angle of the head and the set of the neck and shoulders, even the direction of the person's gaze, are expressive. With a farther viewpoint taking in part or all of the body, he looks for the junctions between shapes – the ways that forms butt together, the angles formed between head, body and limbs, the weight of head on hand or buttocks on chair.

His fascination with these things is not confined to his portrait subjects; he talks about the postures and gestures that describe who people are and how they feel about themselves and the situation they are in: 'People who feel inferior, they take up half a space; confident people take up two spaces.'

The pose, the gestures, lighting, tonality, colour – there are many elements to be juggled in even the simplest portrait. Ken believes that successful results come from knowing the ingredients of your own technique and style, and making them work for you. 'Know your colours – know the palette that you like and use it well; know the face you like and use it well; use everything to your advantage. Basically, it's about doing what you do do well – if you're a greyhound, you run; if you're a bulldog, you stand and fight. Be honest to yourself.'

Cardboard City
535 × 760 mm (21 × 30 in)
This portrait has the kind of rage born of despair. The man's unstoppable momentum is emphasized by the way he is barely contained within the frame, and by the forward thrust of the head. With the head tilted downwards, the direct frontal view leads powerfully on the solid shapes of the brow and nose, and only on those parts of the face has Ken put pure white highlights, delicately touched in by contrast with the colourful masses of the flesh. The fierce, hot red splashed over and behind the head emphasizes the violent mood

MASTERCLASS
with Sally Strand

Sally Strand's paintings are a celebration of the everyday event. You see here ordinary people going about their lives – reading, cleaning, having tea, getting on buses, playing tennis and visiting the beach. If they were snapshots, these images would have a certain charm – but the paintings have a startling impact. Their special vitality comes from the artist's interpretation of her theme through a palette of vibrant lights and colours, beautifully textured by her handling of materials and techniques. The quality of light is Sally's subject on equal terms with the figurative content of the work and for this, pastel is the perfect medium. She organizes her complex, multi-layered surfaces as a synthesis of form and colour, creating the magical impression that the paintings are transmitting their own light. At the same time, she provides a variously witty, serene and touching commentary on daily life that presents to ourselves the way we are.

▶ The Winners
1080×775 mm $\left(42\frac{1}{2}×30\frac{1}{2}\ in\right)$
The light in this painting is particularly strong due to the contrast of tonal values, although there are few extreme dark tones. A gradual weaving of intense, bright but cold colours describes the players' white clothing within the shadowed area. Those blues, greens and mauves are brilliantly complemented by the light-toned yellows that lift the parts in full light. Both elements are enhanced by being set against the deep, warm browns which underlie the flesh tones in the figures and form the background. The shapes create a very rhythmic composition but also a characterful impression of the people

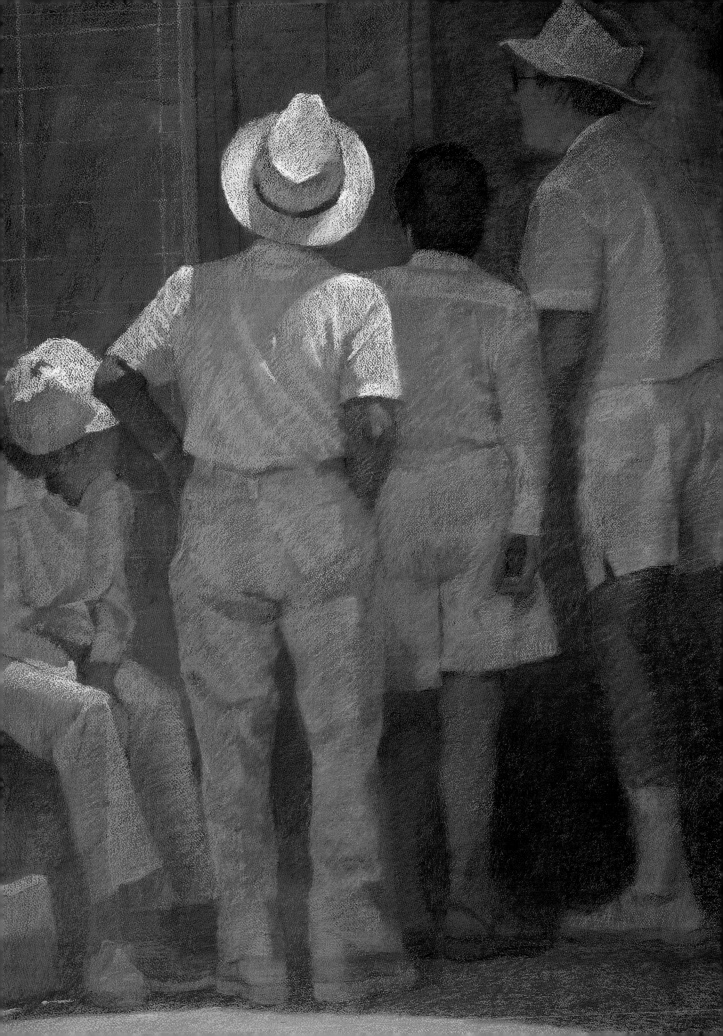

OCTD

660×810 mm (26×32 in)

The strong verticals and solid colours of the bus cut the focus of activity into a very shallow area, so that the sense of depth is mainly directed into the narrow doorway taking the people inside the bus. However, by leaving a sliver of deep space at the front of the bus on the right, Sally has avoided over-emphasizing the horizontal stresses of the composition and has also included there some smaller, more intricate detail that contrasts discreetly with the broader shapes. In fact, although the first impression of movement across and into the pictorial space grabs the viewer's attention, there is a great amount of subtle depth and detail to be discovered more gradually, such as the shadowy shapes in the darkened window

SUBJECT AND IMAGE

A sense of personal association with Sally's human subjects is frankly irresistible. You can identify people just like these among your family and friends, people you see in the street and in other public places. The 'slice of life' element is very strong: each image conveys the mood and incident of a moment in real time, but the narrative is self-contained. You don't need to know where the people are going to when they board the bus in *OCTD*; you are instantly absorbed in that isolated fraction of their 'story'. You have even been part of an incidental grouping such as that described in *Coffee Break*, of people who merely happen to come together in the same place at the same time.

Every viewer is an 'expert' in relation to Sally's subjects, because the situations are familiar and we are all used to reading the body language and gestures of both friends and strangers. It is a truthful kind of

Coffee Break
1040×1270 mm (41×50 in)
The broad horizontal banding of the picture across which the figures sit, each just separated from the next, almost suggests a grid-like underlying structure. But the angles and movements of heads, arms and legs create a dancing motion travelling across the image, despite the sedentary poses. The accompanying photographs (ABOVE) show from where Sally draws her basic references, but also demonstrate how she has changed or combined various elements of form and content and set them in their own context within the composition

a group of men standing all in white; they were lawn bowlers. I did not go there with the intention of painting lawn bowlers – what I saw was a series of patterns, abstract shapes, across the backs of their heads and their shoulders. Abstract shapes in the light, and lots of colours, and reflected light in the shadows, and that's what was interesting to me.'

A SENSE OF CHARACTER

Although Sally certainly enjoys the personalities of her subjects, she is not aiming to create their individual portraits; she works with 'the aura of the person, if you will, trying to say something more about life in general. To get too much into their faces changes the whole intent.' In the paintings, facial features are often no more than subtly suggested. In *Work Day*, for instance, the face is quite abstract, but somehow also an accurate description. However, with her precise eye for shape, colour and texture, and the way light models form, Sally can re-create very explicitly the sense of a person's age and character from all kinds of details other than the face – the weight and balance of a certain posture, the exact contours of limbs, differences of skin texture and colour in old and young people. These elements are beautifully and appropriately varied in her paintings, often by means of surprisingly economical techniques. What she chooses to include about people's clothing and the accessories of their daily lives – hats, newspapers, shopping bags – is also selective and telling.

When she finds a subject in which the personal and painterly interests coincide so well, Sally may work through a series of paintings on that particular theme, getting a train of

Cooler Conference

455×610 mm (18×24 in)
The striking, particular qualities of light always visible in Sally's paintings are here subtly drawn out of a massing of deep, rich tones and colours. With that very vibrant but heavy-toned red at the centre of the composition, the surrounding colours need weight and depth to form a balance. The red is echoed in the hot colours from the underpainting glimmering through the muted greens across the background, and in the strong pink and orange tints applied to the players' faces, arms and hands. The intense blues used in different degrees on the outer figures on either side help to anchor the dynamics of the group, and the court netting provides linear interest at the same time as creating a frame within the frame

expressiveness that she shows us, the pose that describes something fundamental about character and mood. Observe this in *Cooler Conference*: the reason for their animated discussion is not the point, but the posture of each of those men expresses precisely his reaction to what is going on. Sally puts it quite simply: 'I liked what that said about those guys.'

Still, it is important to remember that all these events are filtered through the painter's eyes, and there are other interests at work in both the choice of subject and the interpretation. For example, in a number of the paintings, most or all of the figures are seen from behind. This is intriguing, even challenging to the viewer – people who turn their backs actively exclude you. But the painter is also particularly engaged with the range of shapes and colours contained within the forms, and the patterns of light and shadow that pass across them. 'The first time I painted subjects from behind, it was thought going and exploring different possibilities for composition and technique – changes of scale, colour variations, ways of isolating or grouping the figures and objects. She is not exclusively attached to the human figure, and the 'people paintings' are matched by a number of exceptional still lifes that similarly take ordinary subjects and turn them into extraordinary images. A lovely example is the rhythmic, uncluttered, large-scale composition of *Pear*, in which the fruit's grand, swelling shape achieves a monumental presence – 'it almost takes on a kind of personhood'.

DEFINING THE COMPOSITION

The outdoor subjects are naturally transient, and Sally uses photographic reference as well as drawing from life. She takes colour transparencies and works from them direct by putting them into a slide viewer purpose-designed by an artist that holds the image at eye level and, employing only available light and a mirror, gives a sharp, almost three-dimensional image.

This provides the most versatile use of her references: Sally can take individual elements from a selection of images; turn a slide around to reverse the contours and directions of the shapes; and manipulate the light source to create a different colour cast. In this way, a painting is right from the start an interpretation of the subject, not a re-creation of the photograph: 'Sometimes it turns into a different thing, but I don't want to be caught by projecting the picture, just making it what's already there; I want to make a painting, a piece of work.'

Drawing is a key activity: whether sketching on the spot or working

Pear
850×560 mm $\left(33\frac{1}{2} \times 22\ in\right)$
The scale of the painting puts the pear massively over life size, giving full impact to the monumental quality of its beautiful shape. Sally has left it alone as a dramatic, complete statement by organizing the composition quite flatly, keeping the *background very simple and just bringing in the small corner of patterned fabric at the left to introduce a different kind of visual interest*

Setting the patterns of tonal values for each work is essential preparation for Sally. Although colour intensity is such a striking feature of her paintings, she achieves the effects she is looking for by first becoming very well acquainted with the interplay of tones. She keeps many sketchbooks in which she makes these small pencil drawings

▶ Bowl of Lemons
*355×280 mm (14×11 in)
Sally works on watercolour paper stapled to a board over a layer of newspaper padding. She first masks off the image area on the paper and makes a linear charcoal drawing establishing the basic layout of the composition (1).*

After fixing the drawing, she brushes in the underpainting rapidly and boldly, using acrylic paint applied with large housepainter's brushes (2). The underpainting sets up qualities of colour and texture that she can play against in the pastel painting, and also provides the depth and emphasis of the darker tones that will underpin the vivid qualities of the pastel colour.

Sally uses the side of the pastel initially to glaze broadly across the brushed colour (3). She keys the darkest and lightest shapes, starting to model form and space and orchestrating the vibration of the pastel hues against the underpainting.

The colour builds up into a more complex picture as Sally

from the slides, Sally always draws freehand and lets the images progress freely. For every painting she makes small value sketches in pencil, plotting the patterns of light and dark tones. The essence of her vivid representation of light and colour lies in developing the tonal interpretation effectively. 'I reduce the work to a three- or four-value plan, and if it carries that well when reduced in a pattern, usually it will be bold and strong in the final painting.' This understanding of the tonal balance anchors the colour work: 'I use the sketch as a road map to return to if I get lost in the painting, and it reminds me of what my initial impression was.'

WORKING TOWARDS THE LIGHT

Sally's methods and techniques have evolved towards creating the impact of light and shadow through colour. Her description of light involves the principle of optical mixing – the appearance of colour blends and mixes composed of small strokes and particles of many colours. These

are achieved not by blending the actual substance of the medium on the painted surface, but by building up layers of broken colour that allow the various hues and tones to interact vibrantly.

There are three basic stages in Sally's approach to a painting: she draws up the composition in charcoal on medium-weight watercolour paper, lays in an underpainting in watercolour or acrylic, then starts to apply soft pastel and gradually builds up the surface. The qualities of the materials are important: the paper is firm and has a heavy tooth that keeps the surface open as the pastel is laid on; the charcoal is loose-textured and easy to work and rework, allowing changes in the initial drawing; the paint contributes all-over colour that gives weight and density to the image. Soft pastel is extremely responsive to the underlying textures of paper grain and brush marks, depositing colour on the tiny ridges and mounds but not into the pits of the grain, so that the colours of the underpainting are still seen and the surface remains receptive and workable while the colour overlays are built up gradually.

uses both side strokes and the tip of the pastel to develop form and detail. In this painting, the pastel layers are relatively light, in many areas just gently grazed across the paper grain. The underpainting is very influential in creating the glow of interior light (4).

Rich yellow, orange and purple shades break through the sparkling pastel tints. In the focal point of the painting, the bowl of lemons, the pastel colour is that bit more thickly applied in modelling the fruits, to bring up the local colours and give intensity to the highlighting

The underpainting is freely laid in with large housepainter's brushes, establishing a broad pattern of shapes in rich, subtle hues and tones. It does not directly key the pastel colours; in fact, it often acts as a complement to them and the particular values may strongly counterpoint the colours laid on top. It enables Sally to work with deep, heavy colours – she remarks that one of the few problems she has with soft pastels is that none of the colours is really dark, which, she points out, can make pastel paintings sometimes seem 'too sweet'. Even, say, the more solid browns and purples come up relatively light on application, and using black to darken pure hues would deaden the colour. So

she applies an underpainting that enriches the dark pattern of the composition and makes the overlaid pastel colours 'really sing'.

OVERLAYING COLOURS

Sally begins by working with the side of the pastel, using broken pieces to lay in the large masses – 'I like the phrase, start with the broom and end with the needle.' Her method is a kind of glazing technique, gradually progressing to 'longer sticks and longer strokes, over and under the colours'. In places she moves very lightly over the paper, so that the underpainting maintains a strong presence with glints of pastel colour making the lights – seen clearly in several areas in *Bowl of Lemons*. Elsewhere she may press the pastel more firmly into the grain so the texture develops quite densely. The painting becomes a more and more complex network of laid-on strokes, with underlying colours and textural detail pushing through; it is all an additive process.

Sally tries to avoid making corrections, as erasing loses the freshness and sparkle of the painting. When it is essential, she knocks the colour off with a stiff bristle brush, using a tapping motion. She fixes the painting at every stage, gradually using less fixative on each layer and none at all at the end.

▲ 1

▲ 3

▼ 2

▼ 4

Colour Interactions

The colours in the composition may be suggested by the original subjects, but Sally increasingly makes her decisions according to the painting's progress in its own terms. Using the value sketches when necessary to rekey the tones, she judges the intensity and value of the pastel hues not only to create the light but also to place her focal points and define relationships of form and space.

The effects of broken colour and optical mixing show careful orchestration of harmonies and oppositions – contrasts of hue and tone, and also colour temperature. This is an important factor; often you can see a definite contrast of warm pinks and reds against cold blues and greens, and scintillating yellows set off by low-key mauves, but it is rarely just that simple. You also get sudden flashes of strong colour in the deeper shadows, such as a slash of bright green turning the fold of a garment. Even the subdued shades can have many glorious colour influences in them – Sally mixes subtle olive and sepia tones on the paper, and what she calls 'beautiful greys', made out of woven colour masses that create a muted glow. This applies also to the brightest lights; the brilliantly white clothes of the tennis players and bowlers contain no white pastel – the effect is all achieved through colour mixing.

There is detailed colour interaction all over the surface, not only in each area but also crossing between the shapes, as in *Work Day*. You can see small links and echoes of particular colours cropping up through different elements of the composition, within the overall patterns that model the forms. There again, the complicated areas can be suddenly offset by broad shapes in closely related colours, or the hard-edged opposition of simply stated areas of strong light and deep shadow where there are fewer variations of hue and tone. Nothing is predictable; everything contributes to the pure sensation of colour and light.

▶ Work Day
685×355 mm (27×14 in)
The many objects individually have well-defined, simple shapes but all together build a complex pattern of planes and curves. The activity in the foreground is balanced by the restrained treatment of the background space, with dark tones silhouetting the figure.

The pastel marks have a fairly open texture that enables the viewer to see the variety of colour moving through different elements of the image. Where the contrast of tonal values is most emphatic, the colour oppositions often underline the distinctions between form and space, light and shadow. But within the figure and the objects in her immediate vicinity, there is a more elaborate and delicate crossover of reflected colours and small accents linking through the shapes

MASTERCLASS
with Frances Treanor

The immediate sensation of pure colour is a striking feature of Frances Treanor's work. After specializing in pastel for many years, it is second nature to her to choose it in preference to any other medium, both for its immediacy and for the range of bright primary and secondary colours she can employ. She uses soft pastels of varying brands – her main requirement being that they are not too crumbly – together with harder sticks and pastel pencils to develop detailed areas. She also mixes soft and oil pastels in the large colour areas: putting chalky texture over oil, she obtains a resist technique that 'tears the pigment and creates interesting texture', while oil over chalk provides a vibrant surface effect. Although her orchestration of colours is extremely powerful, it is the way this is married to a strong sense of shape and texture that forms the unique impact and frequently unusual flavour of her compositions.

▶ Irises
1120×810 mm (44×32 in)
This is a favourite subject – the irises grow against the fence in Frances's garden and she works on the paintings outdoors. She responds to their richness by making the most of the strong, fluid shapes and velvety colours, and works hard on creating the right background, using powerful, pure hues rather than the sombre tones of the flowers' natural setting

The Lion's Share

205 × 205 mm (8 × 8 in)
Working on small scale and
using a lighthearted 'naive'
style helps Frances to
overcome the familiarity with
the human figure that she feels
can produce a dull response to
the subject. It also enables her
to illustrate a serious point
obliquely, in a witty manner.
'I title my work with proverbs
from the Bible, Aesop's fables
and wise old women's sayings.
I have fun allowing
imagination to run riot with
uncensored motifs.'
Technically, the bright
colours on white paper and
strong black lines, like a
child's drawing or cartoon, all
contribute to the playful feel

USING COLOUR

Frances's handling of colour goes well beyond conventional notions of how colours interact. You can identify in her paintings the kind of harmonies and oppositions well established in colour theory, which artists have always used knowingly or instinctively, but it is her ability to do the unexpected that makes her skill as a colourist stand out.

In *Animal Magic*, for example, the colours are overall a little more sombre than usual, for reasons that have a practical origin (see caption); the painting contains a range of 'neutrals' – beige and brown, earthy colours – and the pinks, purples and blues are relatively muted. Frances handles these beautifully as a kind of low-key harmony but, unexpectedly, arranges them around a tiny core of jewel-bright colours, the vivid hues of the smaller fruits. These light up the painting, but because the shapes are small and clearly defined, the brightness does not supersede the subtler palette. In a way, there are elements here that could belong to two different paintings, which she has succeeded in unifying with complete conviction.

Animal Magic

495×650 mm $\left(19\frac{1}{2} \times 25\frac{1}{2} in\right)$

In still-life demonstrations carried out away from her own studio, Frances uses props that are portable and durable, such as wicker containers and dried fruits, vegetables and flowers. This painting began in this way, hence the number of elements that contain quiet tones and neutral colours, more muted than the artist's usual range. However, the painting was incomplete at the end of the demonstration and Frances continued to work on it later, developing the imagery in a free, associative way, by extending the forms and colours imaginatively. Introducing her cat as a live model forced her to work quickly, with 'hard, unblended, minimalist strokes'. The result is a delightfully unsentimental 'animal portrait' in a complex, decorative setting

◄ Lilium Regale
1120×810 mm (44×32 in)
The natural grace of the subject is brought to the fore by the sinuous weaving of finely drawn shapes — the stems, leaves and stamens of the lilies and delicate foliage in the foreground. Although these set the rhythms of the composition, their fragile shapes mix with chunkier forms and solid colour areas that provide balance and contrast. The palette is harmonious and restrained, in keeping with the lilies' discreet colouring, but Frances has matched this with a bold, bright-toned border of primary colours that plays strongly against the naturalistic greens and earthy shades

► Spring Rhapsody
1120×810 mm (44×32 in)
The freshness and clarity of this painting is a true celebration of spring. The textures of the materials are used to the full, to make the variety of shape and detail through flat colour areas, hard-edged individual strokes and vibrant colour blends. The surface qualities relate to the forms and tactile qualities of the flowers: notice, for example, the mingled strokes forming the frilled carnation petals and the way the glossy, smooth tulips are rendered with more distinct, solid shapes

In *Lilium Regale* there is a dramatic tonal contrast, with the white flower shapes set against a dark, velvety ground. *Spring Rhapsody* offsets complementary hues and tints – the purples reacting with the strong yellow, the reds with the greens – and Frances makes a bold move in posing the complex flower group against a pale-toned, very actively drawn background. In *Flag Irises* the definition of colour is intensified by the weight and extent of the simplified shapes, and the

relatively limited palette ranges through harmonies and contrasts of tone and hue precisely estimated to form the balance of the painting.

Such confident use of colour is something that cannot be taught. It is a combination of instinct and experience, and many practised artists prefer to stay within much safer boundaries. Pastel is an encouraging medium for experimenting with colour, however. As Frances points out, you do not have to deal with the tiresome practicalities of opening

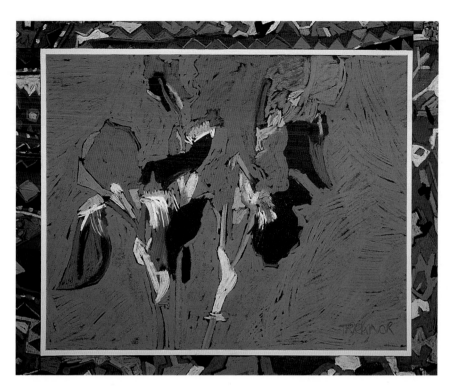

Flag Irises
790×965 mm (31×38 in)
This very close portrait of the iris flowers renders them quite abstractly. Frances simplifies the tonal range to emphasize the dramatic shapes of the flowers. The mid-purple and its blue background are very close in tone, enhancing the striking opposition between the dark violet and the bright flashes of orange and yellow. The broad colour areas give full weight to the lush textures of the pastel strokes

tubes and mixing colours – you can go direct to your colour sensations; but it is essential to remain alert to the way colours change and interact on the paper. When Frances initially sees a strong, dominant hue in the composition, she may take some time trying to match it with her choice of pastel colour. This then acts as a key to the progress of the painting.

SHAPE AND TEXTURE

Some of the more intricate paintings contain a riot of colour. The diversity is anchored by a clear sense of design and expert control of the patterning of shapes. The paintings are quite large-scale, so that individual marks tell significantly. Although the pattern element is often highly active, there is a sharp appreciation of form and space – the shapes of things and the spaces in between them, and the relationship of one object to another in a complex group. The decorative impact of Frances's style could lead the casual viewer to underestimate her rigorous approach to these traditional aspects of composition. As with more strictly representational styles of rendering, she deals continuously with the organization of pictorial space, in terms of shape, tonality, colour values and edge qualities. At the same time, she maintains the level of intense activity right across the picture surface that gives her work its essential character and vitality.

The degree of textural variation is expressed in different ways according to the mood of the composition. Obviously, complex surface activity is inherent in a subject, such as *Lilium Regale* or *Green Man and Disgruntled Daughter*, where there are dozens of component parts of the image; but it is equally present in the large, bold shapes of *Flag Irises* and the rhythmic, internalized construction of *Symbiosis*. These varied surface values come from confident mark-making and a willingness to

124

explore the particular properties of the materials. The soft layering of *Symbiosis* comes partly from rubbing the oil pastel with turpentine; the lines of the composition trail gently through the colour veils. This is a complete contrast to the emphatic linear strokes of grainy soft pastel that activate the shapes in *Spring Rhapsody* or *Animal Magic*.

BORDERS

The collaged borders that surround the large paintings are the result of patient experiment. Technically and visually, Frances had an idea of the effect she was looking for, but she says it took a while to get it right.

There were various reasons for beginning to add the borders. One was simply to extend the painting and make it larger overall; Frances found that mount boards did not suit the images, and were also limited in size. The borders allow her to express two sides of her painterly interests – they are more abstract than the subjects they enclose and enable her to work very freely with colours and shapes, whereas the figurative imagery is anchored by the subject matter. She regards the central image and the border as two individual paintings, and a border can take a long time to complete. Her method of constructing them as collages allows her to change her mind as the work progresses – to vary the visual components in them, or adjust the width of the surround.

Something Fishy
810×1120 mm (32×44 in)
The subject is a brilliant unscaled parrot fish bought from the small tropical range kept by Frances's local fishmonger. She kept it in the freezer to preserve it while drawing. Although this dulls the colours somewhat, Frances exercised her imagination on the delicate patterns that could still be seen. To merge the fish with the background, she utilized a fish-scale motif and floating fish sperm among the underwater plants surrounding it. 'I am intrigued by the fact that species are equipped to survive in adverse conditions through deception and adaptation, hence the title of the painting'

SUBJECT MATTER AND COMPOSITION

Frances is particularly well known for her flower paintings, but the range of work illustrated here demonstrates that they are only one of several interests that she likes to express. *Symbiosis* tackles very directly her strong feelings about the relationships between people through what she describes as 'the ultimate symbiotic relationship' – that between mother and child. The painting explores the artist's relationship with her mother and her daughter, the mutual benefits of such a close attachment and also its painful, 'parasitical' side. The imagery and techniques she has used to develop this personalized theme contrast notably with the approach to the still-life subjects.

Another, yet different approach is seen in *The Lion's Share*, a small, vividly realized oil pastel in which flat colour areas are bounded by strong contour lines initially drawn with a felt-tip pen. Here Frances works quite playfully with the human figure, which she regards as the most powerful image of all but rarely uses directly, because 'its very familiarity can focus my eye too much, because my response is subjective, and the overall effect is portrait-like and dull'. By opting for simplicity of style and technique in this drawing, she achieves an intriguing picture which is also a commentary on 'the unfairness of power-sharing between the sexes'.

This commentary re-emerges obliquely in *Green Man and Disgruntled Daughter*, which visually forms a sort of bridge between the theme paintings and the more direct still lifes. Inspired by the European myth of the Green Man, a symbol of the life force in plants, Frances

decided to explore her own imaginative interpretation. This she did by setting up a still life of fruits and vegetables in the style of the seventeenth-century Flemish school of painting. 'Much to my delight, two faces grew out of the composition. I felt I'd conjured up an image from the metaphysical world – perhaps the female side of Nature, ignored for too long and demanding her say in the myth.'

For the still lifes, Frances 'hoards all kinds of paraphernalia that is unusual and visually striking' – printed fabrics, woven textiles, decorative ornaments, containers and utensils. She often begins with a central group and gradually 'grows' the still life outwards, adding new things as she feels the need to extend the composition. Sometimes she becomes immersed in a passion for the subject that produces a burst of sustained activity, or a practical aspect can set the pace; the irises in her garden, which she paints every year, only last about ten days.

Symbiosis

535×685 mm (21×27 in)
This complex, layered image makes the most of the varying qualities of the materials – oil pastel and soft chalks. Some of the smoother, veiled passages were achieved by rubbing oil pastel with turpentine, a technique used both to obtain the particular texture and to allow Frances to make changes, a form of erasure. The painting is about the intensity of close relationships and also the frequent failures of communication between people. Frances remarks that 'an element of farce in a basically tragic situation helps not to trivialize but to highlight the point', and the imagery of this painting expresses the dark side of the subject matter with a touch of humour

The flower paintings are joyous and beautiful. But Frances is keenly aware that some people are inclined to dismiss flower subjects as 'merely' pretty and decorative, and it is part of her conscious effort to give her paintings a tough, unsentimental character capable of cutting through such a preconception. Her approach to composition, style and technique does have the necessary toughness, underlined by the large scale of the paintings – their impact is enormous.

Green Man and
Disgruntled Daughter
1015×1015 mm (40×40 in)
This personalized exploration of a mythical figure draws on one of the wittier traditions of still-life painting, in which the objects form an 'image within the image'. It also shows Frances further investigating the versatility of the medium, enjoying the different kinds of marks, textures and pattern

qualities that pastel can make, both in the painting and its border. The technical range is highly inventive

ARTISTS' BIOGRAPHIES

Diana Armfield lives in London and in Wales and regularly travels to France and Italy to draw and paint. She is a member of the Royal Academy, the Royal Watercolour Society, the New English Art Club and the Royal West of England Academy. Her work has been exhibited in the UK, USA and Australia, and is represented in several public collections. She has carried out commissions from the National Trust, Reuters, HRH the Prince of Wales and the Contemporary Art Society for Wales. She has also contributed to a number of art books and magazines. (Diana Armfield's pastels are reproduced by courtesy of Browse & Darby, London.)

John Blockley has studios in Gloucestershire and Derbyshire and his paintings often reflect their landscapes, but he enjoys working in a variety of locations. He is President of the Pastel Society of Great Britain, and a member of the Royal Institute of Painters in Watercolours and of the New English Art Club. He exhibits frequently in the UK, particularly in group shows, and has also exhibited in the USA and Germany. His publications include *Watercolour Interpretations* (1987), also published by HarperCollins, as well as two titles in their *Learn to Paint* series: *Pastels* (1980) and *Flowers in Pastel* (1992).

Tom Coates is Vice-president of the Pastel Society, President of the Royal Society of British Artists, and a member of the Royal Society of Painters in Watercolour and of the Royal Society of Portrait Painters. He has had solo exhibitions in the UK and USA, and frequently contributes to group shows. His work has been reproduced in a number of art books and magazines, and he is the author of *Creating a Self-Portrait* (1990). He has carried out several prestigious commissions.

Diana Constance lived and worked in New York, New Mexico and Rome before settling in London. She is a painter and photographer, and has exhibited in solo and group shows in the UK and Europe. Examples of her work are held in several public collections, and she has been featured in various publications and on television and radio in the UK and Germany. She is the author of *Introduction to Painting and Drawing in Pastels* (1990) and *The Life Class* (1991). She teaches at the Camden School of Art, London.

Margaret Glass lives and works in Suffolk and exhibits regularly in the UK, USA and France. Her pastel painting is a full-time commitment and she spends most of each year working towards the major shows arranged for various venues. She is a member of the Pastel Society of Great Britain and of the Societé des Pastellistes de France, contributing annually to their group exhibitions. She is also an Associate of the Societé des Artistes Français and a Fellow of the Royal Society of Arts.

Debra Manifold lives and works near London and her subjects reflect the drama of the urban landscape, in both city streets and public parks. She has exhibited at various London venues, in Ontario, Canada, and also in Paris at the Societé des Pastellistes de France. In the early part of her career she worked as a designer and screenprinter; this experience in design has contributed a powerful graphic impact to her paintings.

Geoff Marsters taught art in secondary schools and colleges until 1986, when he left teaching to work full-time as a professional painter. His paintings frequently feature the landscape surrounding his home in Suffolk, but he also travels widely, notably in France, Italy, Israel and Finland. He has had several solo exhibitions and has contributed to a number of group shows; examples of his work are also held in many private collections in the UK, USA, Europe and Japan.

Ken Paine became interested in portraiture while living and working in the USA. He now lives in Surrey and is a member of the Pastel Society of Great Britain and is Vice-president of the Societé des Pastellistes de France. He has contributed to a wide range of group shows in England, France, the USA and Canada, as well as mounting solo exhibitions in London, and his work is represented in several publications. He has carried out many portrait commissions and is much in demand as a teacher and demonstrator of pastel techniques.

Sally Strand lives and works in California. Her special interest in light and colour is conveyed not only in her own work but in her teaching; she has taught colour theory at Colorado Institute of Art and is a member of the faculty of the Scottsdale Artists' School in Arizona. She has exhibited widely in the USA, being several times selected to contribute to exhibitions held by the Pastel Society of America. Her work has also appeared in many publications and has been featured on US television.

Frances Treanor lives and works in London. She has exhibited in numerous group and solo exhibitions, and has achieved a number of important commissions and awards. She has a very active and varied career: she is involved in several societies (she is a member of the Pastel Society of Great Britain); has taught and lectured in London colleges; and has participated in workshops and demonstrations of pastel techniques. Her work is represented in a wide range of publications.